Learning with Computers

Diana M. Trabel, M.Ed.
Trabel Educational Consulting
Sunman, IN

Jack P. Hoggatt, Ed.D.
Professor of Business Communications
University of Wisconsin
Eau Claire, WI

D1607182

THOMSON
SOUTH-WESTERN

Australia · Canada · Mexico · Singapore · Spain · United Kingdom · United States

THOMSON
SOUTH-WESTERN

Learning with Computers, Level 1
Diana M. Trabel, Jack P. Hoggatt

VP/Editorial Director:
Jack W. Calhoun

VP/Editor-in-Chief:
Dave Shaut

Senior Publisher:
Karen Schmohe

Acquisitions Editor:
Jane Congdon

Development House:
Victory Productions, Inc.

Director Educational Marketing:
Carol Volz

Marketing Manager:
Michael Cloran

Marketing Coordinator:
Linda Kuper

Production Editor:
Martha Conway

Production Manager:
Tricia Boies

Manufacturing Coordinator:
Charlene Taylor

Media Developmental Editor:
Matthew McKinney

Media Production Editor:
Ed Stubenrauch

Design Project Manager:
Stacy Jenkins Shirley

Production House:
Victory Productions, Inc.

Cover Designer:
Brenda Grannan,
Grannan Graphic Design

Cover and Internal Illustrations:
Brenda Grannan

Internal Designer:
Brenda Grannan,
Grannan Graphic Design

Printer:
Quebecor World, Dubuque
Dubuque, Iowa

About the Authors

Diana Trabel has been actively involved in elementary education and computer education for more than 25 years. After ten years as an elementary classroom teacher, Diana brought her classroom experience to curriculum development at South-Western/Thomson Learning. Currently, Diana is an author and educational consultant in the field of computer education. Diana is the co-author of the *Teacher's Resource Guide* for *Bernie's Typing Travels*, a program for teaching keyboarding to elementary students. *Learning with Computers* is the result of Diana's many years of working in education and publishing on how to make computers and software applications accessible and meaningful to all teachers and students.

Dr. Jack Hoggatt has taught Keyboarding at the elementary, middle, and high school levels. He also has taught Keyboarding methods courses and workshops for teachers. Dr. Hoggatt has been an author of South-Western Keyboarding products for the past 18 years, most recently contributing his expertise to *Bernie's Typing Travels*. Dr. Hoggatt is involved with his community and the school activities of his four children.

Dedication

I want to dedicate this book to my husband, Daniel. Without his encouragement and support I would never have reached my goal of becoming a teacher and I wouldn't be writing this book today. My deepest thanks go to some of my "homegrown" testers — my grandchildren — Jessica, Austin, Miranda, and Nichole. Thanks for working through my projects and giving me some great insight and ideas! Diana

Acknowledgements

Comments from reviewers of *Learning with Computers* have been valuable in the development of this book. Special thanks to the following individuals:

Linda Bluth
Roland Park Elementary School
Baltimore, MD

Sherrie James
Springdale High School
Springdale, AR

Vicki Harker
Jefferson-Scranton CSD
Jefferson, IA

Kathy Thorsen
Gurnee School District #56
Gurnee, IL

To the Student

Welcome to *Learning with Computers,* Level 1! In this book, you will find 18 interesting projects that will help you learn how to use the computer.

Several friendly characters will guide you through the steps of each project. Professor Keys, a scientist, will help Jess, a mouse, explain each project.

The book begins with computer basics. You might already know the names of some of the parts of a computer. You will learn more! You will learn to sit the right way and use a computer correctly. Learning how to use the mouse will be so much fun! Then you will learn how to make interesting things with graphics. You will make posters, a bookmark, a mailbox sign, and a colorful place mat.

Have you ever used a word processor? Soon you will be a pro! You will learn how to create and save documents. You will use different fonts, font styles, and font colors. You will cut, copy, and paste, and even add graphics to your documents. Jess will travel with you in a time machine to visit Christopher Columbus. Your word processing skills will help you correct a list of things he had on his ship.

Next, you will learn how to use the Internet to find helpful Web sites. You will use the Internet toolbar and links to move around Web sites to get the information you need.

Projects with spreadsheets and databases are also in this book. Spreadsheets are a fun way to solve math problems. You can use databases to help you keep track of important information.

Each project has a list of computer skills and new vocabulary words. The vocabulary words are also in the glossary at the end of the book. Professor Keys or Jess will give directions for each project. Software screens will help you follow the directions.

A typing lesson in each project will help you develop good keyboarding skills. This keyboarding practice will make it easier to use the computer.

Health and safety are important when using a computer. Jess's friend Jake will introduce ergonomics tips in each project. Pay attention to these tips to build good habits. These tips will even help you when you play video games!

Bernie, Jess's brother, drives a blue convertible named Blueberry. He loves that car! At the end of each project, Bernie and Blueberry will take you on side trips. You will do activities in language arts, math, science, social studies, art, and health.

So join Jess, Professor Keys, Jake, and Bernie! They are ready to teach you all about computers!

CONTENTS

Let's Go!

In this project you will:

- Name computer parts
- Use a computer
- Use floppy disks and CD-ROMs

Word Power

CD-ROM

computer

CPU

floppy disk

keyboard

monitor

mouse

printer

Side Trips with Bernie and Blueberry

Social Studies

Describe Choose a pen pal from the database. Draw a picture of the person. If the pen pal has a pet, draw the pet. Write the pen pal's name on the picture. Write the name of the country where the pen pal lives. Write a sentence about that country.

Language Arts

Write Open your word processor. Write a letter to a pen pal. Tell about yourself. Add a clip art picture or draw a picture.

Parts of the Computer

Professor Keys knows a lot about computers!
She is teaching me. You can learn, too!

What Is a Computer?

The monitor is the screen. A computer screen
is like a TV screen.

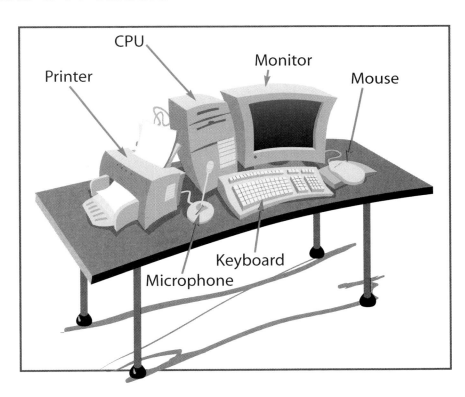

CPU

Printer

Monitor

Mouse

Keyboard

Microphone

Professor Keys' Typing Activities

Open your word processor. Key the drill lines.

b, m, n emphasis

1 nab   men   bin   man   sum   built

2 nab   men   bin   man   sum   built

left shift and period emphasis

3 f.J   K.   L.   U.   I.   O.   M.   N.

4 f.J   K.   L.   U.   I.   O.   M.   N.

left shift emphasis

5 Meg   Meg | Kate   Kate | Jay   Jay

6 Meg   Meg | Kate   Kate | Jay   Jay

left shift sentences

7 Jill   and   Larry   went   home.

8 Jill   and   Larry   went   home.

9 Hal   rode   to   Iowa   with   Jo.

10 Hal   rode   to   Iowa   with   Jo.

The keyboard has letters and numbers. Use it to type words into the computer.

The mouse helps you work with a computer. Use it to point and click.

A cable connects the mouse to the computer. It looks like a tail. That's why we call it a mouse!

I use the printer to print out pictures and letters.

Jake's Ergonomics Tip

Sit straight in front of the computer.
Keep your feet on the floor.

Now let's look at a column. Look at the Country field. There are three pen pals from Mexico.

 Quick Check

Can you tell which pen pals are from Mexico? What are their names?

■ Jose lives in Mexico.

■ Carlos lives in Mexico.

■ Maria lives in Mexico.

Great!

Name	Country
▶ Jose	Mexico
Anna	Canada
Peter	United States
Carlos	Mexico
Sam	United States
Rachel	Canada
Brett	United States
Maria	Mexico
Dan	Canada
Tara	United States

 On Your Own

Look at the database. Find the answer to the riddles.

Lee's pen pal is a girl.

She lives in Mexico.

She has a dog.

Who is she? _____

Jake's pen pal is a boy.

He is 7 years old.

He lives in Canada.

Who is he? _____

 ## Quick Check

Sit at your computer. Let's name these computer parts!

- Where is the monitor? Can you find it?
- Put your fingers on the keyboard.
- Move the mouse.

I use my pointer finger to click on the mouse. Try it!

Part 2

Mind Your Manners

Professor Keys has rules about how to use a computer. Your teacher may have some rules, too. Here are Professor Keys' rules.

Computer Rules

- No drinks or food near the computer!
- No sticky fingers on the keyboard!
- Do not leave disks in the computer.
- Print only when your teacher tells you to print.
- Do not bang on the computer! Ask your teacher for help.

Does your teacher have other rules? What are they?

1. Tap the **Down** arrow key to move to row 2.

This record is all about a pen pal named Anna.

2. Tap the **Right** arrow key.

Anna lives in Canada.

3. Tap the **Right** arrow key.

Anna is a girl.

For AppleWorks, use the **Tab** key.

Name	Country	Boy or Girl	Age	Pet
Jose	Mexico	Boy	5	Dog
Anna	Canada	Girl	6	Fish
Peter	United States	Boy	5	Cat
Carlos	Mexico	Boy	7	Fish

You can use the Right arrow key to move to each field.

Anna is 6 years old. She has a fish for a pet. If Jess writes to Anna, she can ask about Canada. She can ask about Anna's fish.

Jake's Ergonomics Tip

When you use the computer, your eyes should be even with the monitor or just a little bit above the top of the monitor.

Handle with Care

Sometimes I use a floppy disk or a CD-ROM.

Floppy disk

CD-ROM

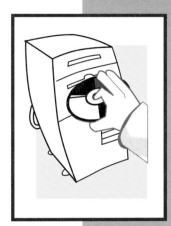

Hold them carefully. Hold them at the edges.

1. Watch your teacher use a CD-ROM.
2. Open the CD-ROM case. Hold the CD-ROM like your teacher does.
3. Put the disk into the disk drive.

Wasn't that easy?

 On Your Own

Look at the pictures your teacher gives you. Each picture shows one part of the computer. Color each part.

This database has ten records. Each record tells about one pen pal. Each row is a record.

Jose	Mexico	Boy	5	Dog
Anna	Canada	Girl	6	Fish
Peter	United States	Boy	5	Cat
Carlos	Mexico	Boy	7	Fish
Sam	United States	Boy	5	
Rachel	Canada	Girl	6	Cat
Brett	United States	Boy	6	Dog
Maria	Mexico	Girl	5	Dog
Dan	Canada	Boy	7	Dog
Tara	United States	Girl	5	Bird

This row is one record. →

Part 3

Getting to Know You

We can find out things about the pen pals. Find the second row. It has the name Anna in the first column.

Name	Country	Boy or Girl	Age	Pet
Jose	Mexico	Boy	5	Dog
Anna	Canada	Girl	6	Fish
Peter	United States	Boy	5	Cat
Carlos	Mexico	Boy	7	Fish

Professor Keys' Typing Activities

Learn: home keys

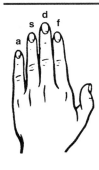  

Meet the Pen Pals

This database has five fields. Each field tells about pen pals.

Name	Country	Boy or Girl	Age	Pet

The fields give information.

- *Name* is the child's name.
- *Country* is the country where the pen pal lives.
- *Boy or Girl* tells if the pen pal is a boy or a girl.
- *Age* tells how old the pen pal is.
- *Pet* tells what kind of pet the pen pal has.

Each column is a field.

Name	Country	Boy or Girl	Age	Pet
Jose	Mexico	Boy	5	Dog
Anna	Canada	Girl	6	Fish
Peter	United States	Boy	5	Cat
Carlos	Mexico	Boy	7	Fish
Sam	United States	Boy	5	
Rachel	Canada	Girl	6	Cat
Brett	United States	Boy	6	Dog
Maria	Mexico	Girl	5	Dog
Dan	Canada	Boy	7	Dog
Tara	United States	Girl	5	Bird

This is the **Name** field.

Professor Keys' Typing Activities

Learn: space bar and enter key

1A.

1B.

1C.

2.

3.
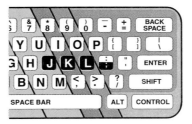

4.

Learn About a Pen Pals Database

Do you know what a pen pal is? Pen pals are people who write to each other. I have a pen pal. Her name is Anna. She lives in Canada. Professor Keys keeps track of our pen pals. She uses a database. I will show you the database. Let's take a look!

Part 1

A First Look

Find the file *pen pals* on your desktop.

Access   **AppleWorks**

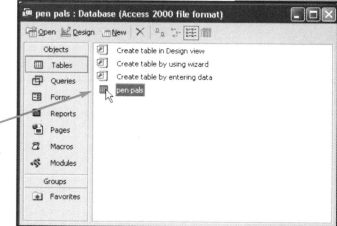

1. Double-click on the icon *pen pals* to open it.

   Access

2. Double-click on the table named *pen pals*.

   Open the *pen pals* table.

Side Trips with Bernie and Blueberry

Art

Draw Draw a picture of your computer mouse. Be sure to include the tail! Tell why it is called a mouse.

Language Arts

Write Write one of the computer rules you learned. Tell why you should follow this rule.

Pen Pals

In this project you will:

- Learn about databases
- Move around in a database
- Use a database to find facts

Word Power

column

database

field

record

row

Ready, Set, Go!

In this project you will:

- Sit the right way at the computer
- Use the mouse
- Use an icon
- Open a program
- Use a button
- Close a program

Word Power

Close box

cursor

desktop

icon

mouse button

screen

word processing program

Side Trips with Bernie and Blueberry

Social Studies

Find Out Choose a job that you like. What kind of tools does a worker need for this job? Does a worker need special clothes? Learn about the job. Use the computer to make a poster. Add clip art or print the poster and draw a picture of the worker.

Language Arts

Write Tell about a job you would like. Open your word processor. Write two sentences about it. Use a capital letter to start each sentence. End each sentence with a period. Add a clip art picture. Print your sentences. Read them to your class.

Use a Computer!

I am going to run a race. I need to warm up so that I do not hurt my body. We can also warm up at the computer. You need to sit the right way when you use a computer. Then your body will not get hurt. I will show you how. Then we will get a good workout as we work on the computer. Let's get started!

Part 1

Sit the Right Way

When you use a computer, you need to sit the right way. I will show you how!

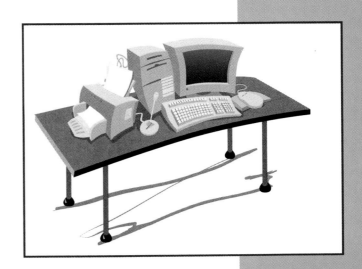

Professor Keys' Typing Activities

Open your word processor. Key the drill lines.

Key: . (period)

all letters learned

1 abd   efg   hijk   lmn   orst   uwy

2 abd   efg   hijk   lmn   orst   uwy

. (period) emphasis

3 l.   l.   .l.   .l.   hr.   ft.   fl.

4 l.   l.   .l.   .l.   hr.   ft.   fl.

5 hwy. hwy. | yd. yd. | ed. ed.

6 hwy. hwy. | yd. yd. | ed. ed.

7 s.a   k.b   n.d   j.e   g.f   a.g   .

8 s.a   k.b   n.d   j.e   g.f   a.g   .

9 h.k   i.s   j.u   o.m   r.n   w.s   .

10 h.k   i.s   j.u   o.m   r.n   w.s   .

Look at the picture.

Wrists are low.
Don't touch
the keyboard.

Monitor is at
eye level.

Feet are flat on
the floor.

Back is
against
the chair.

Now it is your turn.

- Is your back against the chair?
- Are your feet on the floor?
- Are your arms away from the keyboard?
- Is your monitor at eye level?

If your feet do not touch the floor, use a footrest or a stack of books.

Print It!

Find the Print button on the toolbar.

1. Click on the **Print** button.

Remember to wait for your paper to come out of the printer.

We are all done.

On Your Own

Let's color some jobs! Use the database you printed out. Look at the *Where* field. Find two records with *hospital*. Color them red. Find the record with *bakery*. Color it yellow.

Moving Day

In class, you keep books on your desktop. Your computer screen has a desktop. My computer desktop looks like this.

If your computer is a Mac, your desktop may look like this.

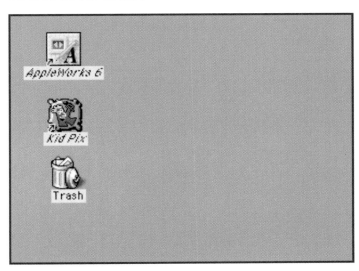

Now let's look at the *Where* field. You see two
records that say "hospital." That means
that two people work at the hospital.

Who	What Job	Where
Tim	carpenter	workshop
Li	teacher	school
Ben	nurse	hospital
Kate	doctor	hospital
Mike	police officer	all over town
Ana	farmer	farm
Ho	firefighter	all over town
Pablo	factory worker	factory
Will	baker	bakery
Sally	mail carrier	all over town

Can you tell who they are? You are right! Ben
and Kate work at the hospital.

Ben	nurse	hospital
Kate	doctor	hospital

A computer desktop has little pictures.
They are called icons.

Microsoft Word

1. Find the word processing icon. It might look like this.

When you move the mouse, you should see the cursor or arrow move.

Let's use the mouse to move an icon.

2. Put your hand on the mouse.

3. Place the cursor on the *My Computer* icon.

4. Press the mouse button with your pointer finger.

5. Click on *My Computer*.

When the icon changes color, you know you have got it!

6. Hold down the mouse button.

7. Drag the icon to a new place on your desktop.

Wow! You are doing a great job with your mouse!

Jake's Ergonomics Tip

Always sit straight at the computer. Keep your elbows close to your body.

Good Work

Let's look at the database. Find the third row.
It has the name *Ben* in the first column.

1. Use your **Down** arrow key to move down to row 3.

For AppleWorks, use the **Tab** key.

A row is a record. This record is all about Ben.

Who	What Job	Where
Tim	carpenter	workshop
Li	teacher	school
Ben	**nurse**	**hospital**
Kate	doctor	hospital

2. Tap the **Right** arrow key.

Ben is a nurse.

3. Tap the **Right** arrow key.

Ben works in a hospital.

Find the record for Will. What is his job?

Pablo	factory worker	factory
Will	**baker**	**bakery**
Sally	mail carrier	all over town

Will is a baker.
He works in a bakery.

Click, Click

Are you having fun? Let's open the word processing program. Are you ready?

1. Double-click on the word processing icon.

Look at the top right corner of the window. Do you see these small boxes?

Word   AppleWorks

2. Click on the circled box.

Did your window get smaller or bigger?

3. Click on it again.

Did your window go back to the same size? This box is the Restore Down button.

> *On some computers, you only have to click once to open a program. How many times did you have to click to open your program?*

A database has records. A record
is in a row. There are 10 records.
Each record tells about one worker.

Who	What Job	Where
Tim	carpenter	workshop
Li	teacher	school
Ben	nurse	hospital
Kate	doctor	hospital
Mike	police officer	all over town
Ana	farmer	farm
Ho	firefighter	all over town
Pablo	factory worker	factory
Will	baker	bakery
Sally	mail carrier	all over town

This row is
one record.

Jake's Ergonomics Tip

Take a break and give your eyes a rest.
Look away from the monitor. Look at
something across the room. Look out the
window. Do not let your eyes get tired!

Find the box with the X. This is the Close box. It is next to the Restore Down button. When you click on the Close box, your program will close. Ready?

Word

If you do not have a box with an X, find the box in the left corner. It looks like this.

4. Click on the **Close** box.

You should be back at your desktop. Good work!

 On Your Own

Click on another icon. Move it to a new place on your desktop. Super! You know how to use your mouse!

Good Jobs

This database has three columns. Each column is called a field.

Who	What Job	Where

There are three fields.

- *Who* tells us the person's name.
- *What Job* tells the job that the person does.
- *Where* tells us where the person does the job.

Who	What Job	Where
Tim	carpenter	workshop
Li	teacher	school
Ben	nurse	hospital
Kate	doctor	hospital
Mike	police officer	all over town
Ana	farmer	farm
Ho	firefighter	all over town
Pablo	factory worker	factory
Will	baker	bakery
Sally	mail carrier	all over town

Professor Keys' Typing Activities

Open your word processor. Key the drill lines.

all letters learned

1 jl   fa   sd   ks   jd   ks   la   fa   j

2 jl   fa   sd   ks   jd   ks   la   fa   j

3 kak   jsj   ldl   fjf   aka   dld   s

4 kak   jsj   ldl   fjf   aka   dld   s

5 a   a | as   as | ask   ask | all   all

6 a   a | as   as | ask   ask | all   all

7 add | add | fall | fall | jak   jak

8 add | add | fall | fall | jak   jak

9 lass   lass | sad   sad | ad   ad

10 lass   lass | sad   sad | ad   ad

Use a Database About Jobs

We had Job Day at school today. We learned all about jobs. People in our town have many kinds of jobs. Some people help others. Some people make things. We are making a list of jobs. We are using a special table. It is called a database. Would you like to learn more? Great! We can use a database now.

Part I

Off to Work We Go

First let's open the database.

Access   **AppleWorks**

1. Double-click on the icon *workers* to open the file.

   Access

2. Double-click on the table named *workers*.

Open the *workers* table.

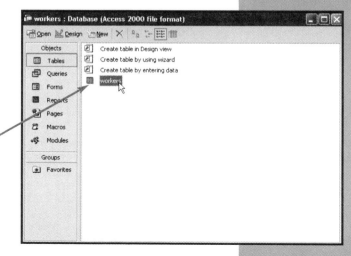

Side Trips with Bernie and Blueberry

Health

Exercise When you work at a computer, take short breaks and stretch.

Hands Make a fist. Now, spread your fingers apart as far as you can. Do this a few times.

Neck Tilt your head to the side. Do not lift your shoulder. Count to ten. Then tilt your head to the other side.

Shoulders Open your arms wide. Roll your shoulders forward five times. Now roll them backward five times. Make wide circles with your arms!

Wrists Hold one hand out. Use your other hand to gently press down on it. Do you feel your muscles in your arms stretching?

Use these warm-up exercises often. Have fun!

All Kinds of Workers

In this project you will:

- Learn about databases
- Move around in a database
- Use a database to find facts

Word Power

column

database

field

record

row

Starry Nights

In this project you will:

- Open a file
- Save a file
- Name a file
- Use a Line tool
- Use the Fill Color tool or Color palette button

Word Power

Color palette button

Color Picker tool

draw tools

Fill Color tool

Line tool

toolbar

Side Trips with Bernie and Blueberry

Math

Vote Imagine it is a VERY rainy day. What would be your favorite thing to do?

- Read
- Play with blocks
- Do a puzzle
- Play cards
- Draw or color

Your teacher has started a chart on the board. It is called "Favorite Things to Do on a Rainy Day." There are 5 rows on the chart. Vote for your favorite thing to do. The rest of your class will vote, too. Make a table on a piece of paper like the one Jess made in this project. Count to see which one got the most votes.

Connect the Stars

At school, we are learning all about the stars. Some stars are in groups. These groups are called constellations. My favorite constellation is the Big Dipper. It looks like this! Come help me connect the stars! I will show you how.

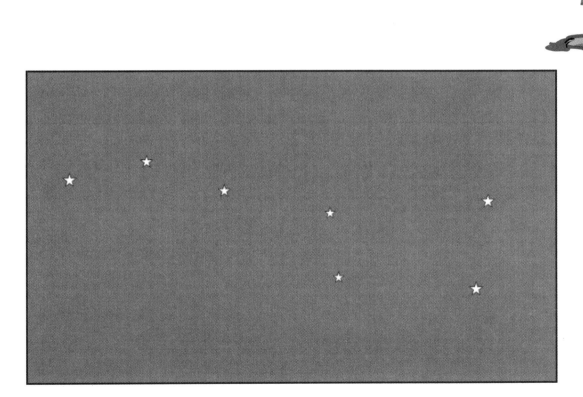

Professor Keys' Typing Activities

Open your word processor. Key the drill lines.

Review

g emphasis

① go   gas   eggs   gain   gift   gold

② go   gas   eggs   gain   gift   gold

w emphasis

③ what   where   wink   was   jewel

④ what   where   wink   was   jewel

m emphasis

⑤ most   time   mind   metal   milk

⑥ most   time   mind   metal   milk

b emphasis

⑦ ball   blue   build   bill   book

⑧ ball   blue   build   bill   book

y emphasis

⑨ eyes   today   yell   daily   yet

⑩ eyes   today   yell   daily   yet

Getting Started!

Let's open my file and get started!

1. Double-click on the icon named *stars*.

Word

AppleWorks

Kid Pix

You will see this window.

Word

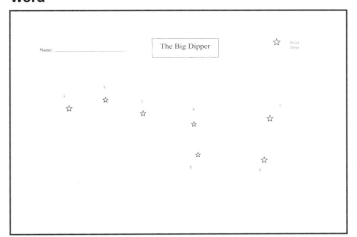

AppleWorks

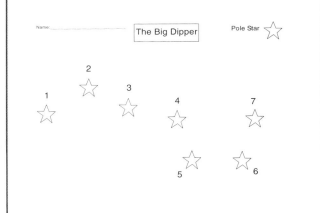

Kid Pix

Count how many oranges are on the tray.

3. Type *4* in the cell.

4. Tap **Enter**.

Count how many bananas are on the tray.

5. Type *3* in the cell.

6. Tap **Enter**.

You have done a lot of work! Let's save it!

7. Click on the **Save** button to save your work.

✓ Quick Check

Does your spreadsheet look like this?

	Fruit		
	Fruit	**How Many**	**Count**
	🍎 Apple	6	· · · · · ·
	🍓 Strawberry	12	· · · · · · · · · · · ·
	🍐 Pear	5	· · · · ·
	🍊 Orange	4	· · · ·
	🍌 Banana	3	· · ·

❋ On Your Own

Print your spreadsheet. Color each row the color of the fruit.

Now let's save the file with a new name.

2. Click on the **Save** button.

Word

AppleWorks

Kid Pix

3. Click at the end of the word *stars* in the **File name** box.

4. Type *3*.

5. Click on the **Save** button.

OK! Now we can start connecting the stars!

Jake's Ergonomics Tip

You are using the mouse a lot in this project. Here is an exercise you can do for your wrists. Draw circles in the air with your pointer finger. You can move your wrists, but keep your elbows and upper arms still.

Now let's count how many strawberries are on the tray.

There are 12 dots.

5. Type *12* in the cell.

6. Tap **Enter**.

7. Click on the **Save** button to save your work.

Way to go! You are doing a great job!

Still Counting!

You are really good at working with spreadsheets. Now let's finish this one. Ready?

Count how many pears are on the tray.

1. Type *5* in the cell.

2. Tap **Enter**.

	A	B	C
1		Fruit	
2	Fruit	How Many	Count
3	🍎 Apple	6	· · · · · ·
4	🍓 Strawberry	12	· · · · · · · · · · · ·
5	🍐 Pear	5	· · · · ·
6	🍊 Orange		· · · ·
7	🍌 Banana		· · ·

AppleWorks

Connect the Stars

We will use some draw tools.

Line tool

Your toolbar may look different, but it will work the same way.

Kid Pix

Click here to get the **Line** tool.

Word

Line tool

We can draw a line from star 1 to star 2. We will use the Line tool. It is very easy!

When you click on the Line tool, the cursor may change to a plus sign.

Word	**AppleWorks**	**Kid Pix**
Line tool	**Line** tool	**Line** tool

1. Click on the **Line** tool.
2. Place the cursor (+) at **star 1**.
3. Click and drag the cursor to **star 2**.

That is where you type the number that tells how many apples are on the tray.

Count the dots in the next cell.

Point to them and count.

Did you count 6 dots?

There are 6 apples.

3. Type *6* in the cell next to the word *Apple*.

4. Tap **Enter**.

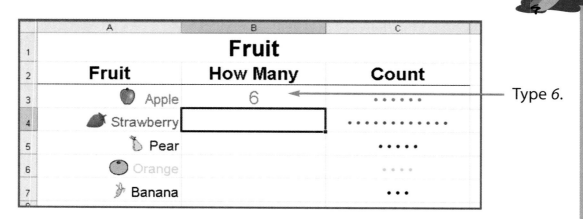

Type 6.

Jake's Ergonomics Tip

How are you sitting at the keyboard? Your back should be against the back of the chair.

This is great. Now we can connect stars 2 and 3.

4. Click on the **Line** tool.

5. Place the cursor next to **star 2**.

6. Click and drag to draw a line from **star 2** to **star 3**.

OK! Now let's finish our constellation. Follow the same steps to connect stars 4, 5, 6, and 7.

7. Click on the **Save** button.

Word   AppleWorks   Kid Pix

 Quick Check

Does your Big Dipper look like this? Give yourself a pat on the back! You have done great work!

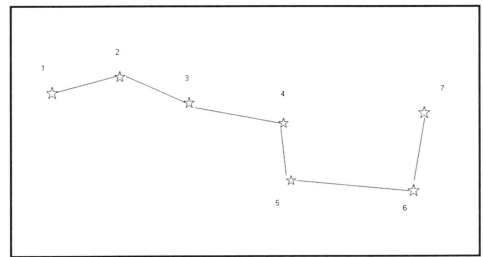

Look at my spreadsheet about fruit. The first column lists all the different kinds of fruits on the tray. A column is a line of cells going from top to bottom.

Each row is about a different kind of fruit. A row is a line of cells going from side to side.

column

	A	B	C
1		Fruit	
2	Fruit	How Many	Count
3	Apple		• • • • • •
4	Strawberry		• • • • • • • • • • • •
5	Pear		• • • • •
6	Orange		• • • •
7	Banana		• • •

row

Part 2

Fruit Roundup

Now we can put numbers in the rows. Let's count the dots in each row.

1. Click your mouse on the word *Apple*.
2. Tap the **Right** arrow key. [···→]

It will move the cursor to the next cell.

Dazzle with Colors!

Let's change the color of the stars in our constellation. It is so easy! We can use a tool to fill a shape with color.

 **Word and AppleWorks**

1. Click on **star 1**.
2. Click on the arrow in the **Fill Color** tool or the **Color palette** button.

Word　　Click on the arrow.

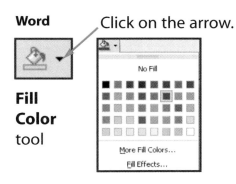

Fill Color tool

AppleWorks　　Click on the arrow.

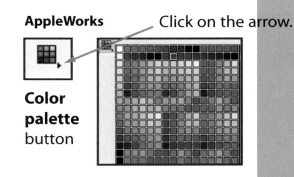

Color palette button

3. Click on a blue color.

 Kid Pix

1. Click on the **Paint Bucket** tool.
2. Click on the **Color Picker** tool.
3. Click on a blue color.
4. Click on **star 1**.

Kid Pix

Color Picker

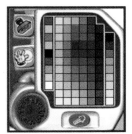

A Tray of Fruit

Let's open the spreadsheet. Then we will save it with a new name.

Excel   **AppleWorks**

1. Find the file *fruit* on your desktop.
2. Double-click on it to open it.
3. Choose **Save As** from the **File** menu.
4. Click at the end of the word *fruit* in the **File name** box.
5. Type *16*.

Type
16.

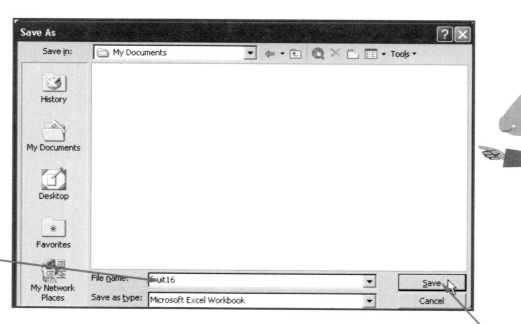

Click on the
Save button.

6. Click on the **Save** button.

You are getting really good at saving files!

Let's make star 6 and star 7 blue too.

 Word and AppleWorks

4. Click on **star 6**.

5. Click on the tool to add color.

6. Repeat the steps to make **star 7** blue.

Let's make star 2 red.

7. Click on **star 2**.

Now we need to change the color from blue to red.

8. Click on the arrow in the **Fill Color** tool or **Color palette** button.

9. Click on a red color.

Looking good! Let's save our work now.

 10. Click on the **Save** button.

Part 4

Star Light, Star Bright

We can color the rest of the stars. Let's make star 3 red too.

 Word and AppleWorks

1. Click on **star 3**.

2. Click on the tool to add color.

In **Kid Pix**, just click on the stars to make them blue.

In **Kid Pix**, click on a color and then click on a star.

Fruit in a Spreadsheet

My grandmother gave us fruit today.

Bernie and I counted each kind of fruit.
We used a spreadsheet to make a chart.

I need to put in the numbers.
Numbers in a spreadsheet are called data.
Will you help me? It will be fun!

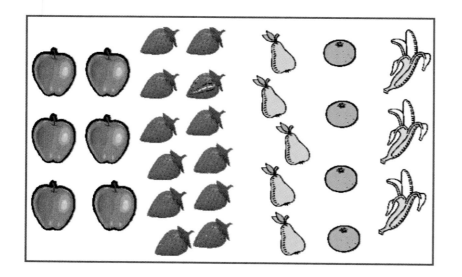

Let's make stars 4 and 5 yellow.

3. Click on **star 4**.

4. Click on the arrow in the **Fill Color** tool or **Color palette** button.

5. Select a yellow color.

6. Click on **star 5**.

7. Click on the tool to add color. It should still be yellow.

8. Click on the **Save** button.

In **Kid Pix**, remember to click on a color and then click on the stars.

All

✓ Quick Check

Does your constellation look like this?

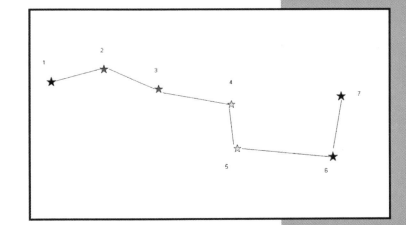

✳ On Your Own

Keep working on the file *stars3*. Connect stars 4 and 7. Change the color of three stars. Pick a color you like.

Fruit from Grandma

In this project you will:

- Use a spreadsheet
- Move your cursor in a spreadsheet
- Add data to a spreadsheet

Word Power

column

data

row

spreadsheet

Professor Keys' Typing Activities

Open your word processor. Key the drill lines.

Review: e, i, o

e emphasis

1 e ef ej ea el ed ek es ej

2 e ef ej ea el ed ek es ej

i emphasis

3 i if ij ia il id ik is ij

4 i if ij ia il id ik is ij

o emphasis

5 o of oj oa ol od ok os oj

6 o of oj oa ol od ok os oj

e, i, o emphasis

7 fee fee | look look | did did

8 fee fee | look look | did did

9 aid aid | sea sea | sold sold

10 aid aid | sea sea | sold sold

Side Trips with Bernie and Blueberry

Health

Games List games you play at recess. Vote for the game you like best. Ask your friends to vote, too. Add the votes for each game. Tell which one is the favorite game.

Language Arts

Movies Make a list of movies you and your friends have seen. Vote for your favorite movie. Ask each friend to vote, too. Add the votes to see which one is the favorite movie.

Side Trips with Bernie and Blueberry

Color Do more work on the file *stars3*. Type your name at the top of the page. Change the colors of the stars.

Find Out Here is a picture of the Little Dipper. Draw the Little Dipper. The end of the handle is the Pole Star. Find out more about the Pole Star. Tell your class about the star.

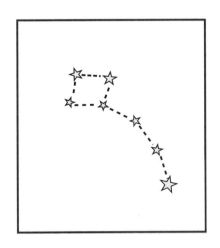

Professor Keys' Typing Activities

Open your word processor. Key the drill lines.

Key: y

all letters

1 job fen hug walk sad trim

2 job fen hug walk sad trim

y emphasis

3 jy jy yjy yjy yd yw yl yn

4 jy jy yjy yjy yd yw yl yn

5 guy guy | say say | yarn yarn

6 guy guy | say say | yarn yarn

7 sky sky | day day | yell yell

8 sky sky | day day | yell yell

9 yet yet | you you | year year

10 yet yet | you you | year year

My Five Senses

In this project you will:

- Add clip art
- Resize clip art

Word Power

clip art

resize

sizing handles

Close the Spreadsheet

We are all done.

We can close the spreadsheet now.

1. Click on the **Close** button.

2. If a window pops up to save it, click on **No**.

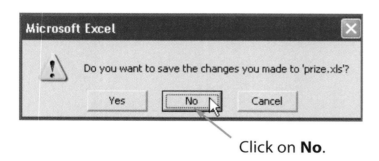

Click on **No**.

On Your Own

Jess and two friends voted for Games. If two more friends vote for Games, how many votes will there be all together?

Add Clip Art to a Poster

Do you know what our five senses are? They are sight, smell, taste, touch, and hearing. I am making a poster about the five senses. Will you help me add pictures to my poster? Let's get started!

Part I

Getting Started

Let's open my poster.

Word	AppleWorks	Kid Pix

1. Double-click on the file *senses* on your desktop.

You will see my poster. Before we work on this file, let's save it.

2. Select the **File** menu and choose **Save As**.

3. Click at the end of the word *senses* in the **File name** box.

4. Type *4*.

5. Click on the **Save** button.

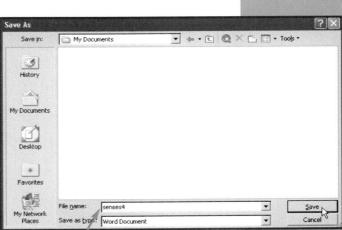

Type *senses4* in the **File name** box.

 **Quick Check**

■ Which prize got the most votes? It is the favorite prize.

■ How many votes did it get?

■ Which prize got the least votes?

■ How many votes did it get?

	A	B	C	D
1	Our Class Reward			
2	Prize	How Many	Count	
3	Popcorn	5	• • • • •	
4	Movie	7	• • • • • • •	
5	Games	3	• • •	
6	Recess	4	• • • •	
7				

Good Tastes

The computer has lots of pictures. We call pictures on the computer clip art or clippings. Let's find clip art of something good to eat! Apples taste good! Let's add clip art of apples.

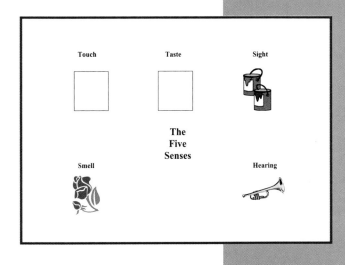

 Word and AppleWorks

1. Click on the box under the word *Taste*.

 2. Click on the clip art button.

Word	AppleWorks	Kid Pix
Clip art button	Clippings button	Stickers button

 Word and AppleWorks

3. Click in the search box.

4. Type *apples*.

5. Click on the **Search** button.

6. Double-click on the picture you like.

Word

Type *apples*. Click on the **Search** button.

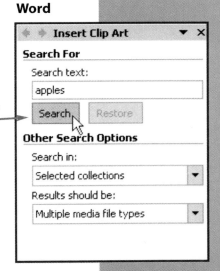

Find the Answers

We can use the spreadsheet to answer questions. Which prize is the favorite? The spreadsheet can tell us.

Look at the row with *Popcorn*.

2	Prize	How Many	Count
3	Popcorn	5	• • • • •

What is the number in that row? There are five dots to show 5. That is the number of votes for popcorn.

Look at the row with *Movie*.

4	Movie	7	• • • • • • •

There are seven dots to show 7. That is the number of votes for movies.

3. Find the sticker **Folder name** box.

4. Click on the little green triangle to find *Food*.

5. Click on the picture of fruit.

6. Drag the picture into the box under the word *Taste*.

Great! You added clip art!

Word	AppleWorks	Kid Pix

7. Click on the **Save** button.

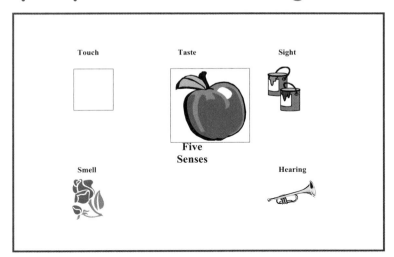

✔ Quick Check

Does your poster look something like this?

Touch   Taste   Sight

Five
Senses

Smell   Hearing

Jake's Ergonomics Tip

Remember to keep your feet flat on the floor
or on a block. Keep your back straight and
against the back of your seat.

2. Tap the **Right** arrow key. ⟶

C5	▼	*fx* • • •		
	A	B	C	D
1	Our Class Reward			
2	Prize	How Many	Count	
3	Popcorn	5	• • • • •	
4	Movie	7	• • • • • • •	
5	Games	3	• • •	
6	Recess	4	• • • •	
7				

There are three dots to show 3.

There are three dots to show three votes.

Jake's Ergonomics Tip

Sit close, but not too close to your keyboard. Put one hand between you and the keyboard. That's right! Now you know how to sit at the keyboard.

Big or Small?

Look at the clip art of the apples. Does it fit? You can resize the clip art to make it bigger or smaller. It is easy. I will show you how!

1. Click on the picture.

Now you see a box with little dots. We call the dots sizing handles.

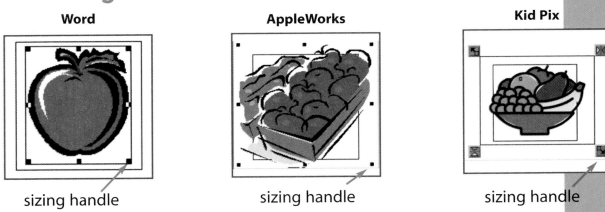

Word   AppleWorks   Kid Pix

sizing handle   sizing handle   sizing handle

2. Place your cursor on a sizing handle.

The cursor changes to an arrow.

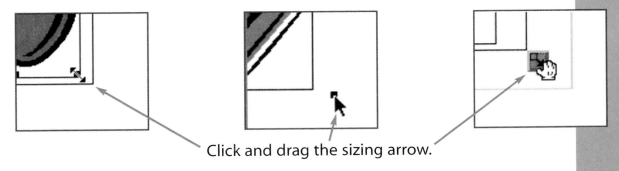

Click and drag the sizing arrow.

3. Click and drag the bottom right sizing arrow.

Up, Down, Left, Right

You can move around in the spreadsheet. You can use the arrow keys.

Use the arrow keys to move to the word *Games*.

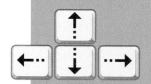

A5 ▾	*fx* Games		
	A	B	C	D

1	Our Class Reward		
2	Prize	How Many	Count
3	Popcorn	5	• • • • •
4	Movie	7	• • • • • • •
5	Games	3	• • •
6	Recess	4	• • • •

Go to this cell.

When you go to a cell, you see a line around it. The cell is selected.

1. Tap the **Right** arrow key.

You have moved over to the next cell.

B5 ▾	*fx* 3		
	A	B	C

1	Our Class Reward		
2	Prize	How Many	Count
3	Popcorn	5	• • • • •
4	Movie	7	• • • • • • •
5	Games	3	• • •
6	Recess	4	• • • •

This cell is selected.

Now the selected cell is the blue *3*.

Drag the handle down and to the right to make the picture bigger.

Drag the handle up and to the left to make the picture smaller.

4. Make the picture fit in the box under the word *Taste*.

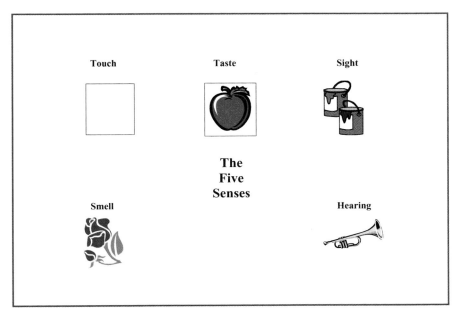

5. Click on the **Save** button.

Word

AppleWorks

Kid Pix

Great work! You added and resized clip art!

Part I

Prize List

Let's look at our spreadsheet.

1. Find the file *prize* on your desktop.
2. Double-click on the icon *prize* to open it.

The spreadsheet shows what we voted for.

Excel

prize

AppleWorks

prize

	A	B	C	D
1	Our Class Reward			
2	Prize	How Many	Count	
3	Popcorn	5	• • • • •	
4	Movie	7	• • • • • • •	
5	Games	3	• • •	
6	Recess	4	• • • •	
7				

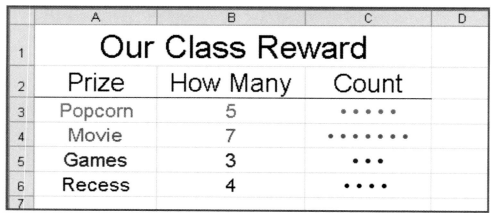

row

column

Project 15   **143**

A Soft Touch

You did a great job adding clip art! Let's add more. Let's find a picture for the sense of touch. Let's look for a picture of a cat. A cat has soft fur.

Word and AppleWorks

1. Click on the box under the word *Touch*.

2. Click on the clip art button.

Word and AppleWorks

3. Click in the search box.

4. Type *cat*.

5. Click on the **Search** button.

6. Double-click on the clip art you want.

Word

Type → cat.

AppleWorks

Type cat.

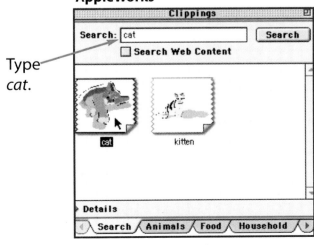

Use a Spreadsheet

Professor Keys is proud of all our hard work! We get to pick a prize.

We can have a popcorn party, watch a movie, play games, or have an extra recess.

We all voted for the prize we want. Now I want to count the votes. We can use a special table to count the votes. It is called a spreadsheet.

A spreadsheet looks like this.

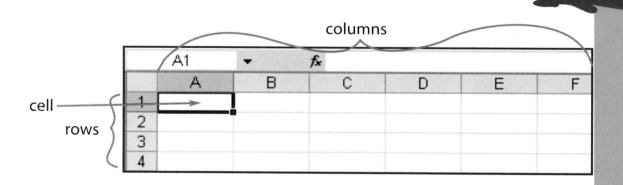

Each box is called a cell. The boxes that go across make a row. The boxes that go down make a column.

Kid Pix

3. Find the sticker **Folder name** box.

4. Click on the little green triangle to find *Animals*.

5. Click on the picture of a cat.

6. Drag the picture into the square under the word *Touch*.

Resize your clip art if you need to.

7. Click on the **Save** button.

Super job! That was fun!

 Quick Check

Does your poster look something like this?

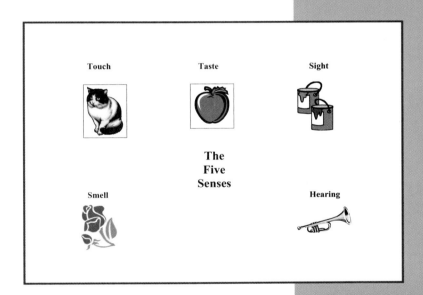

Touch   Taste   Sight

The
Five
Senses

Smell   Hearing

 On Your Own

Choose one of the five senses. Add another clip art picture to that sense. Save the file as *my senses4*.

Make Your Vote Count!

In this project you will:

- Learn about spreadsheets
- Move to cells
- Use the arrow keys

Word Power

cell

column

row

spreadsheet

Professor Keys' Typing Activities

Open your word processor. Key the drill lines.

t emphasis

1 t tf tj ta tl td tk ts te

2 t tf tj ta tl td tk ts te

n emphasis

3 n nf nj na nl nd nk ns ni

4 n nf nj na nl nd nk ns ni

t emphasis

5 to to | font font | take take

6 to to | font font | take take

n emphasis

7 fin fin | join join | nail nail

8 fin fin | join join | nail nail

t, n emphasis

9 ton ton | knot knot | toe toe

10 ton ton | knot knot | toe toe

Side Trips with Bernie and Blueberry

Social Studies

Map Double-click on the *E-Patrol* icon. Look at the map of North America. Draw a map like this on a piece of paper. Draw two animals that live in North America on your map.

Science

Make a Poster Double-click on the *E-Patrol* icon. Learn more about one of the animals. Use a drawing program or your word processor to tell about the endangered animal.

Side Trips with Bernie and Blueberry

Science

Animals Open your word processor. Think of all the animals you know. Add clip art of three animals. Print your paper. Share your paper with your class. Tell what you know about each animal.

Health

Good Food What food makes you strong and healthy? Open your word processor. Type *Good Food* at the top of the page. Add clip art of good food to eat. Save your file as *food4*.

Professor Keys' Typing Activities

Open your word processor. Key the drill lines.

all letters learned

1. hum   jell   disk   after   wagon
2. hum   jell   disk   after   wagon

b emphasis

3. fb fb bfb bfb bj bi bd bw
4. fb fb bfb bfb bj bi bd bw

5. bed bed | bat bat | ball ball
6. bed bed | bat bat | ball ball

7. bit bit | jab jab | blue blue
8. bit bit | jab jab | blue blue

all letters learned

9. me   dog   few   hut   jars   blink
10. me   dog   few   hut   jars   blink

Fire Safety

In this project you will:

- Create and name a file
- Use special keys
- Add a picture
- Resize a picture
- Change the font size and color

Word Power

font
Font Color button
Font Size button
Shift key
Space Bar
Text Color button
text insertion point

You will see this Web page.

North America

Click on a picture to learn more.

Click here.

2. Now click on the picture of the whale.

Read about the alligator. Good work! You can go to pages on a Web site!

On Your Own

Click on the Back button two times. Scroll down. Click on another continent link. Then click on one picture. What animal did you find?

Make a Fire Safety Poster

A firefighter visited Jess's school today. Now Jess needs your help to make a fire safety poster. You can use the computer. Come along and I will show you how!

Part I

Getting Started

Before we begin, I want to tell you about some special keys.

1. Find the **Space Bar** on your keyboard.

We use the Space Bar to put a space between words.

> SPACE BAR

We use the **Shift key** to make capital letters.

2. Find the **Shift** key. There are two of them on your keyboard.

> Shift

To make a capital letter, hold down the Shift key as you type.

Finding Your Way

**Oops! We forgot to click on the last picture.
It is easy to find the pictures again.
We can use the
Forward button.**

Click on
the
Forward
button.

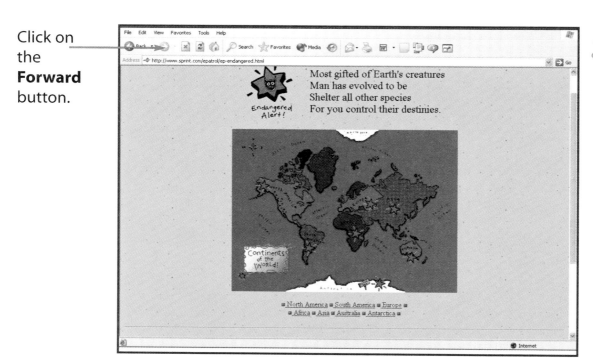

1. Click on the **Forward** button.

Now we are ready to make our fire safety poster.

1. Double-click on the word processor icon on your desktop.

Word

AppleWorks

AppleWorks: Click on the **Word Processing** icon in the **Starting Points Window**.

This opens up a blank document. It looks like a sheet of paper.

At the top of the page you can see the text insertion point. It looks like a flashing line. This is where we will put the title for our poster.

Text insertion point

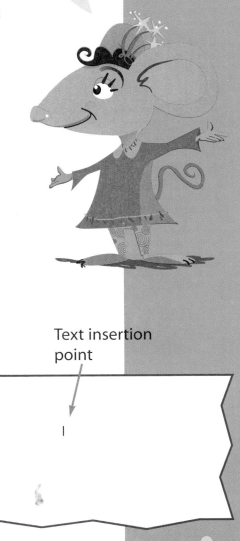

You will see this Web page. It tells about the bald eagle.

Bald Eagle

This majestic bird nests along sea coasts, major waterways and lakes. Dining mostly on fish, the bald eagle builds large nests on the tops of trees or on cliffs. Eagles return to the same nest year after year. Although these birds live a long life and lay two eggs every year, more die every year than are born. Destruction of trees and contamination of the bald eagle's prey by toxic chemicals are the main causes of this incredible bird's decline. Many projects are helping protect these eagles and they have recently been removed from the endangered species list to the "threatened" list.

7. Click on the **Back** button.

8. Click on the third picture. It looks like a turtle.

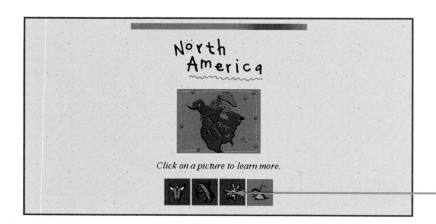

Click on a picture to learn more.

Click here.

You will see this Web page. It tells about the cougar.

Cougar

The largest of North American cats, mountain lions, also known as pumas or cougars are known for their loud piercing scream. Extremely agile cats, they can leap up to a ledge or tree branch more than 16 feet off the ground. Preferring rocky terrain, cougars will travel over a hundred miles stalking deer. Hunted heavily by man, the Eastern and Florida cougar are now near extinction.

9. Now click the **Back** button two times.

Now we are back where we started!

2. Type *Fire*.

Hold down the Shift key when you strike the letter *F*.

3. Tap the **Space Bar**.

4. Type *Safety*.

Hold down the Shift key when you strike the letter *S*.

5. Click on the **Save** button on your toolbar.

Word

AppleWorks

6. Type *Fire Safety5* in the **File name** box.

7. Click on **Save**.

Type *5* at the end of *Safety*.

Click on **Save**.

When the window pops up in Word, it will say Fire Safety *in the* **File name** *box. Type* 5 *at the end of* Safety.

You will see this Web page.

Let's read about bison. *Bison* is another word for *buffalo*.

Bison

At one time, the American Bison wandered the plains of North America in herds of millions. However, bison were extinct in the wild by the late 1800's due to hunting by European settlers. Bred in captivity since this time, their numbers now stand at between 30 and 50 thousand. These massive animals can weigh up to 3,000 pounds and reach 6 feet at the shoulder.

Now let's go back to the Web page we were just on. It is very easy! We can use the Back button.

5. Click on the **Back** button on the Internet toolbar.

6. Now click on the second picture. It looks like an alligator.

Click here.

Part 2

Picture This!

Now we can add a picture to our poster.

1. Tap the **Enter** key 5 times.

Let's find some clip art for fire safety!

2. Click on the clip art button.

Word

AppleWorks

3. Click in the search box.

4. Type *firefighter*.

5. Double-click on a picture you like.

Jake's Ergonomics Tip

Sit up straight. Do not slouch. Stop every now and then to stretch your arms. Reach up to the sky. Reach out far and wide!

You will see this.

Find the words *North America*. The words are underlined. The words are a hyperlink or link.

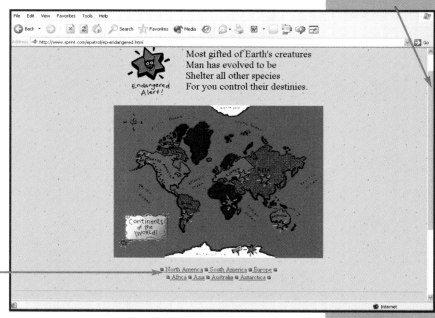

Click and drag the scroll bar.

Click on the link *North America*.

The link will bring you to a new page.

2. Put your mouse on the link *North America*.

3. Click once.

Click and drag the scroll bar to see all of the links.

You will see this Web page. Find the four pictures.

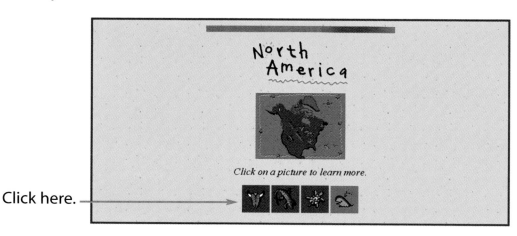

Click here.

4. Click on the first picture.

Now the picture is on the page. Make it fit.

6. Click on the sizing handles to make the picture bigger or smaller.

Word   **AppleWorks**

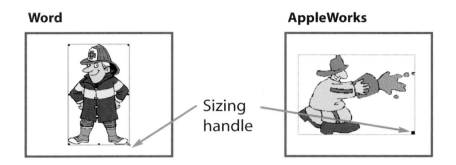

Sizing handle

7. Click on the **Save** button on your toolbar.

Great job!

 **Quick Check**

Does your poster look something like this?

Fire Safety

Find Out About Animals

Jess is learning about endangered animals. These are animals that we need to protect. We must take care of the places where they live.

The blue whale is an endangered animal. It lives in the ocean. Let's use the Internet to help Jess learn more about other endangered animals.

Save the whales

Part I

The Search

We will go to a Web site.

Word

E-Patrol

AppleWorks

E-Patrol

1. Double-click on the icon named *E-Patrol*.

Jake's Ergonomics Tip

Remember to sit up straight when you use a computer. Then you will not hurt your shoulders and neck.

Part 3

Big and Bright

Let's make the words stand out. First we will make the words really big. To change the font size of the letters in a word, we can use the Font Size button on the toolbar.

1. Double-click on the word *Fire*.

The letters look different now. The word is *selected*.

2. Click on the small black arrow on the **Font Size** button.

The number tells how big the letters are.

3. Scroll down to the number *36* and click on *36*.

Do you see how big the word *Fire* is now?

Find the Animals

In this project you will:

- Look at a Web site
- Click on links to go to Web pages
- Use the Back button
- Use the Forward button

Word Power

Back button

Forward button

hyperlink

link

Web page

Web site

Save the whales

Let's color the word. We can use the Font Color button or Text Color button.

4. Click on the arrow on the **Font Color** or **Text Color** button.

Word

AppleWorks

5. Click on the color red.

The word *Fire* is now big and red! Let's make the word *Safety* big and bright too.

6. Double-click on the word *Safety*.

7. Click on the **Font Size** arrow and choose *36*.

8. Change the color, too. Pick any color you want.

9. Click on the **Save** button.

Good work! You made a poster!

Side Trips with Bernie and Blueberry

Science

Read Work with a partner to see more pages on the Kids Earth & Sky Web site.

1. Double-click on the icon named **Kids Earth & Sky**.
2. Click on the **Kids Activities** link.
3. Click on the **Science Quizzes** link.
4. Click on the **Bugs** link.
5. Take the quiz.
6. Click on the **How'd I do?** button.
7. Read how you did.

Art

Draw Draw a picture of the sun on the computer. Then type a poem about the sun. Think about how the sun makes you feel. Think about why we need the sun. Then write your poem.

 **Quick Check**

Does your Fire Safety poster look something like this?

Fire Safety

 On Your Own

Let's add something to our safety poster. Open the file *Fire Safety5*.

At the top of the page, type *911*. This is the number you call if you need help. Make *911* extra big. Add another picture to your poster.

Professor Keys' Typing Activities

Open your word processor. Key the drill lines.

all letters learned

1 jail   desks   right   won   muff

2 jail   desks   right   won   muff

m emphasis

3 mini   milk   mist   mold   merge

4 mini   milk   mist   mold   merge

w emphasis

5 wash   will   wise   wait   wheel

6 wash   will   wise   wait   wheel

u emphasis

7 use   rust   undo   turns   under

8 use   rust   undo   turns   under

g emphasis

9 go to get | glad to get the

10 go to get | glad to get the

Professor Keys' Typing Activities

Open your word processor. Key the drill lines.

Key: r

all letters learned

1 n   ej   ia   tk   di   so   lf   dn   eo

2 n   ej   ia   tk   di   so   lf   dn   eo

r emphasis

3 fr   fr   rfr   rfr   rk   rk   rj   rj

4 fr   fr   rfr   rfr   rk   rk   rj   rj

5 r | for for | are are | far far

6 r | for for | are are | far far

7 ran ran | jar jar | sore sore

8 ran ran | jar jar | sore sore

all letters learned

9 it   to   ask   for   tin   dad   jello

10 it   to   ask   for   tin   dad   jello

6. Then close the Internet window.

Fantastic! I have had lots of fun exploring the Internet with you!

 **Quick Check**

- Where do you find Web pages?
- What happens when you click on a link?
- How do you print a Web page?

*Click on the **Close** box to close the window. You can also choose **Exit** or **Quit** from the File menu.*

 On Your Own

Connect the stars on your paper. Color the picture. Have fun!

Side Trips with Bernie and Blueberry

Language Arts

Write Here are two very important safety rules. Open your word processor. Type the rules. Use the right end punctuation. Start each sentence with a capital letter. Change the font size and color of each sentence. Add clip art.

- If the house is on fire, get out quickly.
- Never enter a burning building!

My favorite holiday is Thanksgiving!

Social Studies

Draw Make a poster about your favorite holiday. Type the name of the holiday at the top of the page. Add clip art. Type one sentence that tells why you like this day.

Very good! We can now print the picture of the constellation Leo. Ready? Let's go! Find the Print button on the Internet toolbar.

4. Click on the **Print** button.

If you cannot see the Print button, click on the "See more" button on the Internet toolbar. Select Print from the pull-down menu. »

Now let's close the Internet window. It is very easy! First close the window showing the constellation Leo.

5. Click on the **Close** button. **Close** button

Close button

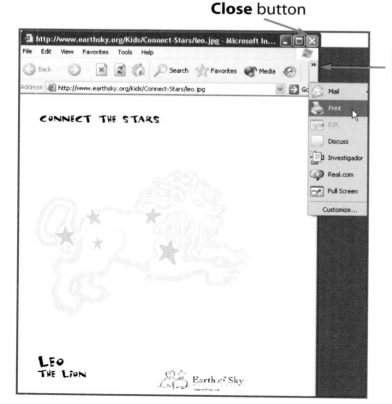

See more button

Pretty Bookmarks

In this project you will:

- Create a file
- Name a file
- Save a file
- Use draw tools
- Add a picture

Word Power

Fill Color tool

Rectangle tool

Now let's look at some of the pictures.

2. Scroll down until you see the pictures of the constellations.

They look like this.

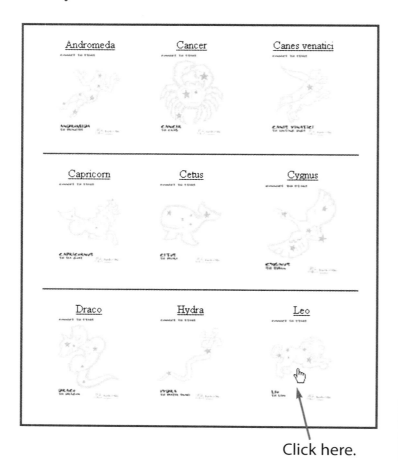

Click here.

3. Click on the picture of Leo.

A new window opens. It looks like this.

Each picture has a link.

Draw a Bookmark

I love to read! I am reading a funny story.
I need a bookmark to keep my place.
We can use the computer to make a
bookmark. You can make one with
me! I will show you how. Let's go!

Part I

Tool Time

Let's start by making a new file.

1. Double-click on one of these icons on your desktop.

Word   **AppleWorks**   **Kid Pix**

AppleWorks

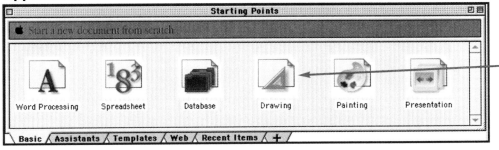

Select the **Drawing** program.

A Friendly Lion

This Web site has pictures of constellations.
Each group of stars has a name.
Let's find out more!

1. Click on the <u>Connect the Stars!</u> link.

You will see this Web page.

Click on
**Connect
the Stars!**

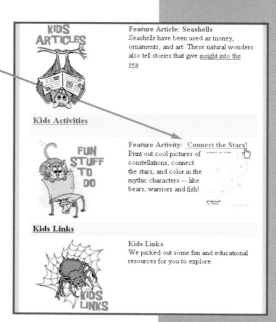

Your window should look like one of these.

Word

Drawing toolbar

Rectangle tool

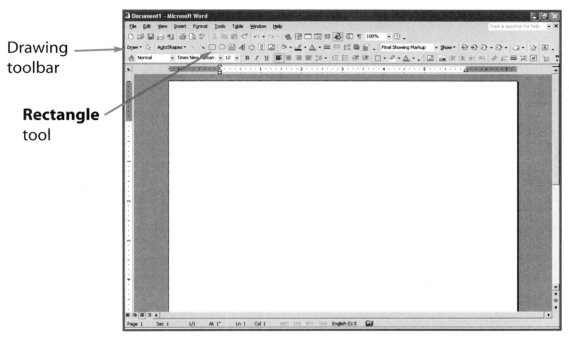

Kid Pix

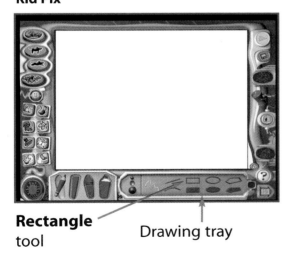

Rectangle tool

Drawing tray

AppleWorks Drawing

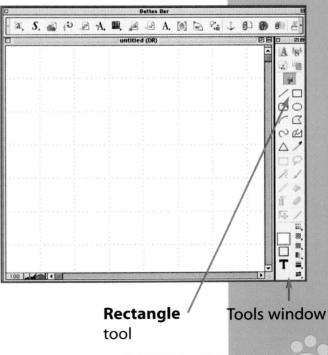

Rectangle tool

Tools window

Now let's use the scroll bar. We will find a link to another Web page on this Web site. Ready? Let's go!

2. Click on the scroll bar and drag it down until you see Kids Activities.

This is what it looks like.

You are doing a great job. Let's explore some more!

Most links are blue and underlined.

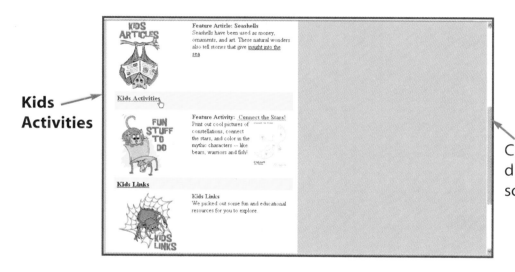

Kids Activities

Click and drag the scroll bar.

Jake's Ergonomics Tip

Your monitor should be right in front of you. You should not turn your head to see the monitor. You should not look up or down at your monitor. Some monitors can be moved or tilted. Can yours?

Let's draw a bookmark that we can cut out.
A bookmark looks like a tall narrow rectangle.
We will use the Rectangle tool on our toolbar.

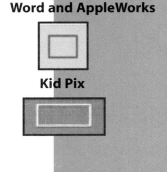

2. Click on the **Rectangle** tool.

Your cursor may change to a plus (+) sign.

3. Place your cursor near the top of the page.

4. Click and drag to draw a rectangle.

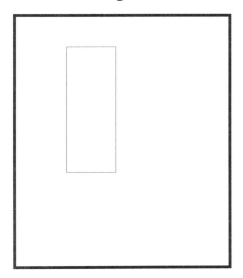

Be sure to make the bookmark tall and narrow.

Let's save our bookmark now!

5. Click on the **Save** button on the toolbar.

Word   AppleWorks   Kid Pix

6. Type *bookmark6* in the **File name** box.

7. Click on **Save**.

The World Wide Web

Would you like to learn about the stars? We can use the Internet. We can go to a Web site. A Web site has pictures and much more. Let's go to the Internet and find a picture of some stars!

Part I

Searching for Stars

I found a Web site called *Kids Earth & Sky*. It tells about groups of stars called constellations.

1. Double-click on the icon named *Kids Earth & Sky*.

You will see this window. It shows the Web site *Kids Earth & Sky*.

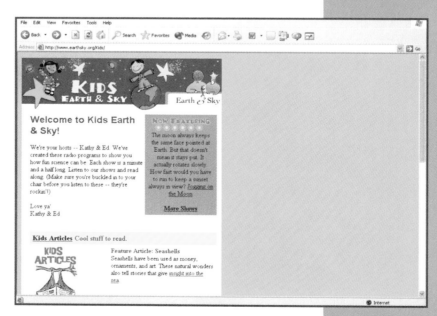

A Colorful Reminder

We can fill the bookmark with a color. We will use draw tools.

Word

Fill Color tool

AppleWorks

Color palette button

Kid Pix

Color Picker tool

Click on the black arrow on the Fill Color tool or Color palette button to pick a color.

1. Click on the bookmark.
2. Fill it with a color you like.
3. Click on the **Save** button.

Your bookmark is very colorful now!

 Quick Check

Your bookmark should look something like this.

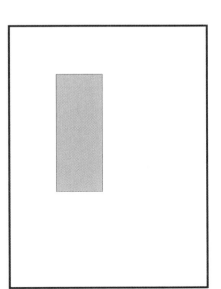

Connect the Stars

In this project you will:

- Look at a Web site
- Click on links to go to Web pages
- Use a scroll bar
- Print a Web page

Word Power

Internet

Internet toolbar

link

scroll bar

Web page

Web site

Pretty Pictures

Let's add a picture! We can add clip art. Let's add a ball.

1. Click on the clip art button.
2. Type *ball* in the search box.
3. Double-click on the one you like.

*Kid Pix: Click on the **Stickers** button.*

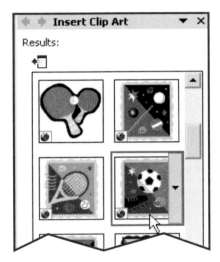

I chose the soccer ball!

Jake's Ergonomics Tip

Pretend you have a golf ball in the palm of your hand when you type. This will help you remember to keep your fingers curved. Keeping your fingers curved is the right way to type.

Side Trips with Bernie and Blueberry

Art

Create Open your word processor. Type these words on your computer.

- buzz
- zip
- rainbow
- pop

Use different font styles and colors for each word. Then add a picture for each word. When you find the clip art you want to use, place it next to the word. Save your file as *words12*.

Language Arts

Story Pictures What is your favorite story? Open your word processor. Type some words of things that are in the story. Look for clip art. Add clip art that matches your story words. Save your file as *story12*.

Word

The clip art will be behind the bookmark.

4. Click on the clip art.
5. Click on the **Text Wrapping** button.
6. Choose **In Front of Text**.

 Now change the size of your clip art.

1. Click and drag a sizing handle to make the clip art bigger or smaller.
2. Click and drag the clip art onto the bookmark.
3. Click on the **Save** button.

Super job!

 Quick Check

Does your bookmark look something like this?

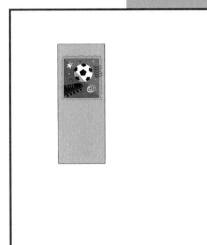

 On Your Own

Add another picture to your bookmark. You can change the color of your bookmark, too!

Professor Keys' Typing Activities

Open your word processor. Key the drill lines.

Key: m

all letters learned

1 w hn gt oi ur ef dj sk al

2 w hn gt oi ur ef dj sk al

m emphasis

3 jm jm mjm mjm mt mr ml mi

4 jm jm mjm mjm mt mr ml mi

5 mitt mitt | mail mail | me me

6 mitt mitt | mail mail | me me

7 jam jam | milk milk | arm arm

8 jam jam | milk milk | arm arm

all letters learned

9 think jails gum fork weed

10 think jails gum fork weed

Professor Keys' Typing Activities

Open your word processor. Key the drill lines.

Key: h

all letters learned

1. r nl id os ef kj ta nt ro
2. r nl id os ef kj ta nt ro

h emphasis

3. jh jh hjh hjh hn hr hs hk
4. jh jh hjh hjh hn hr hs hk

5. h | the the | hot hot | hit hit
6. h | the the | hot hot | hit hit

7. hi hi | hide hide | half half
8. hi hi | hide hide | half half

all letters learned

9. do it he ton ask jar fill
10. do it he ton ask jar fill

 **Quick Check**

Your list should now look like this!

Your name

Vowels

Words with Long Vowels	**Words with Short Vowels**
be	bet
say	sad
note	not
ice	if
ate	at
cute	cut

You made some pretty cool changes! Great job!

 **On Your Own**

Add clip art to your list of words. Put the cursor at the end of the list. Add a piece of clip art.

Side Trips with Bernie and Blueberry

Art **Draw** Use your drawing program. Make a bookmark about your favorite book. Add a picture about something in the story.

Math **Count** Use your drawing program. Make three rectangles. Fill two rectangles with the color blue. Fill one rectangle with the color yellow. Add the number of rectangles. Type the sum.

$$2 + 1 = 3$$

Wonderful! Now let's change the color of the words with short vowels. They are black. Let's make them green!

6. Double-click on the word *bet*.
7. Click on the arrow on the **Font Color** or **Text Color** button.
8. Click on a green color.

The word *bet* changes color from black to green.

Good job! Let's finish up!

9. Double-click on the word *sad*.
10. Click on the **Font Color** or **Text Color** button.

The word *sad* changes from black to green.

Repeat these steps until all the words with short vowels are green.

11. Click on the **Save** button.

My Mailbox

In this project you will:

- Create, name, and save a file
- Use toolbar buttons
- Change the font size
- Add a picture
- Cut, copy, and paste pictures

Word Power

Copy button

Cut button

Paste button

toolbar

Word

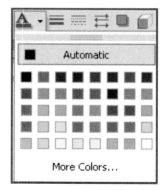

AppleWorks

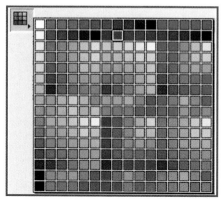

Word: The bar under the A *in the* **Font Color** *button changes color when you pick a new color!*

3. Click on a blue color.

The word *be* is now blue.

Let's try another word!

4. Double-click on the word *say*.

5. Click on the **Font Color** or **Text Color** button.

The word *say* changes color from black to blue.

Repeat these steps until all the words with long vowels are blue.

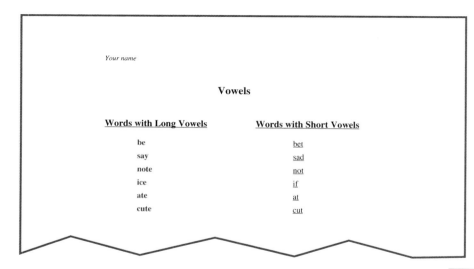

Your name

Vowels

Words with Long Vowels	Words with Short Vowels
be	bet
say	sad
note	not
ice	if
ate	at
cute	cut

Draw a Mailbox Sign

We have a new mailbox in front of our house. Could you help me make a sign for it? The sign will show the number of my house. It is 5191. The sign will show my last name. My last name is Mouse. Come on! We can work together!

Part I

Home Sweet Home

Let's get started. First we need to create a new file.

1. Open your word processor or drawing program.

Word	AppleWorks	Kid Pix

*AppleWorks: Click on the **Drawing** icon in the **Starting Points** window.*

Colorful Words

Now let's change the color of the words in our list. Ready?

Let's look at the toolbar again. We will use the Font Color button or Text Color button to apply color. Find it on your toolbar now.

Word

Italic button

Bold button   **Underline** button   **Font Color** button

AppleWorks

Italic button

Text Color button   **Bold** button   **Underline** button

First, let's change the color of the words with long vowels. They are black. We want them to be blue. Let's give it a try!

1. Double-click on the word *be*.
2. Click on the arrow on the **Font Color** or **Text Color** button.

You will see a window that looks like one
of these.

Word

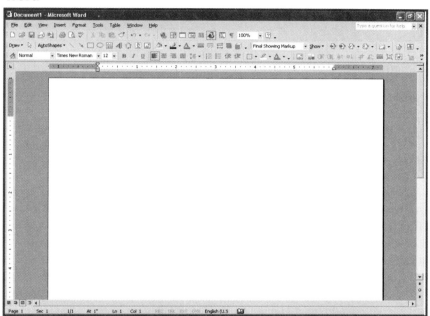

AppleWorks

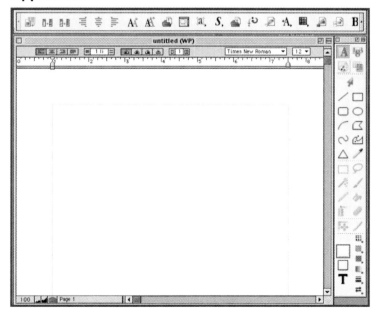

Kid Pix

Short Lines

Great work! Now let's underline the words with short vowels. We will use the Underline button.

1. Double-click on the word *bet*.
2. Click on the **Underline** button.
3. Double-click on the word *sad*.
4. Click on the **Underline** button.

Repeat these steps until all the words with short vowels are underlined.

5. Click on the **Save** button.

 Quick Check

Does your list look like this? If not, make your changes now.

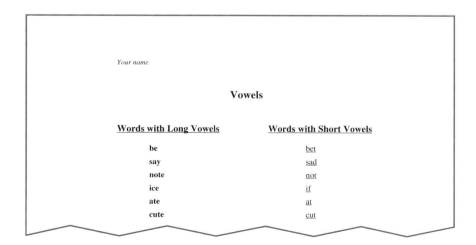

Your name

Vowels

Words with Long Vowels	Words with Short Vowels
be	bet
say	sad
note	not
ice	if
ate	at
cute	cut

First, let's save the file. We can name it too.

2. Click on the **Save** button on your toolbar.

Word

AppleWorks

Kid Pix

A window like this appears.

3. Type *mailbox7* in the **File name** box.

4. Click on the **Save** button.

OK! We are ready now. This will be fun!

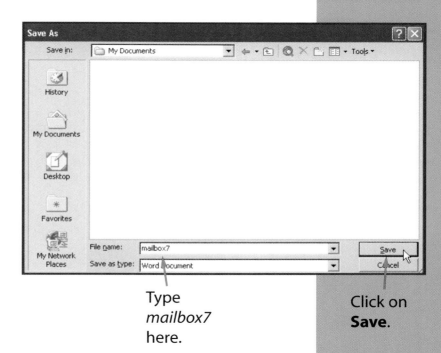

Type
mailbox7
here.

Click on
Save.

Jake's Ergonomics Tip

Your body will get tired if you work at the computer too long. Take a break every 15–20 minutes. Wiggle your fingers. Shake your hands. Stand up on your tiptoes!

Quick Check

Your list should look like this. If not, make your changes now.

Your name

Vowels

<u>Words with Long Vowels</u>	<u>Words with Short Vowels</u>
be	bet
say	sad
note	not
ice	if
ate	at
cute	cut

Jake's Ergonomics Tip

Make sure your monitor is at eye level. Do not look up or look down. Look straight ahead. Sit on some books if you are too low.

Number and Name, Please

**Let's type the number of my house.
Then we will type my last name.**

1. Place your text insertion point at the top of the page.

2. Type *5191*.

3. Tap **Enter** three times.

4. Type *Mouse*.

5. Tap **Enter**.

6. Click on the **Save** button.

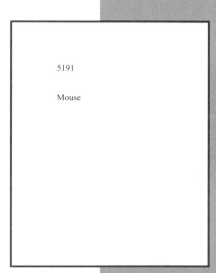

Let's make the number and name really big. We want the mail carrier to see them! We will use the Font Size button.

7. Double-click on *5191*.

8. Click on the **Font Size** button and choose *36*.

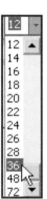

No one could miss this big number!

5191

The word *be* should now be bold.

Your name

Vowels

Words with Long Vowels   **Words with Short Vowels**

Words with Long Vowels	Words with Short Vowels
be	bet
say	sad
note	not
ice	if
ate	at
cute	cut

Let's keep going.

3. Double-click on the word *say*.
4. Click on the **Bold** button.

Now you know how to use the Bold button!

Repeat these steps until all the words with long vowels are bold.

5. Click on the **Save** button.

9. Double-click on *Mouse*.

10. Click on the **Font Size** button and choose *36*.

11. Click on the **Save** button.

Word	AppleWorks	Kid Pix

 Quick Check

Does your sign look big too?

5191

Mouse

Sign Design!

Let's make a picture! I want to add some clouds and a tree and a bird. We can use clip art.

Kid Pix: You can also use the **Stamp** *button!*

1. Click on the clip art button.

Word	AppleWorks	Kid Pix

Clip Art	**Clippings**	**Stickers**

2. Click in the search box.

3. Type *tree*.

4. Double-click on a picture you like.

Now let's change the style of your name. We will use the Italic button. Ready?

3. Double-click on your first name.
4. Click on the **Italic** button.

5. Now double-click on your last name.
6. Click on the **Italic** button again.

Good job! Let's save your work now.

7. Click on the **Save** button.

When you double-click on a word, the word is selected.

Part 3

Bold Words

Now let's use the Bold button. We can make all the words with a long vowel sound bold. It is easy to do! I will show you how.

1. Double-click on the word *be*.
2. Click on the **Bold** button.

5. Resize the picture so it fits.

6. Now add a picture of some clouds.

7. Resize it to fit.

8. Now add a picture of a bird.

9. Resize it to fit.

10. Click on the **Save** button.

Fantastic work! You are getting good at adding clip art!

 Quick Check

Does your mailbox sign look something like this?

Click on the sizing handles. Drag the handle to resize the picture.

5191

Mouse

Cool Changes

We are going to have fun with this list! First we will change the font style. Some font styles are bold, italic, and underline.

We will use buttons on the toolbar.

Word

Italic button

Bold button   **Underline** button   **Font Color** button

AppleWorks

Italic button

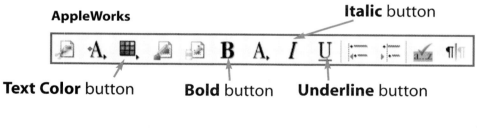

Text Color button   **Bold** button   **Underline** button

- **This is bold style.**
- *This is italic style.*
- <u>This is underline style.</u>

1. Click at the top of the page.
2. Type your name.

Lots of Trees

I like my mailbox sign. I like the picture of the tree. I will copy my tree. Then I will have two trees. You can copy a picture, too.

This is the Copy button. It lets you copy shapes and pictures.

Word	AppleWorks	Kid Pix

This is the Paste button. It lets you put copies of shapes and pictures where you want.

Word	AppleWorks	Kid Pix

This is the Cut button. It lets you cut out any shapes and pictures that you do not want.

Word	AppleWorks	Kid Pix

1. Click on the tree.
2. Click on the **Copy** button.
3. Click on the **Paste** button.

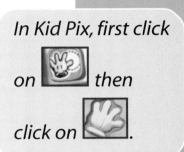

In Kid Pix, first click on *then click on* .

Add Style to a List

I am learning about long vowels and short vowels. The word *me* has the long vowel sound. The word *met* has the short vowel sound. Say the word *me*. Now say the word *met*. Do you hear the difference?

I have a list of words with long and short vowel sounds. Let's change the way the words look. Come with me!

Part I

Sound Them Out

Let's open my list of words.

Word   **AppleWorks**

1. Double-click on the icon named *vowels*.

Before we make any changes, let's save our file.

2. Choose **Save As** from the **File** menu.

3. Type *vowels12* in the **File name** box.

OK! Now we are ready to add style!

4. Click on the sign.

5. Drag your new tree where you want it.

6. Click on the **Save** button.

What do you think of our sign so far?

 Quick Check

Does your mailbox sign look something like this?

5191

Mouse

Sometimes the copy of the picture covers the old picture. Click and drag it.

Short and Long Vowels

In this project you will:

- Use the toolbar buttons
- Change the style and color of words

Word Power

Bold button

Font Color button

Italic button

style

Text Color button

Underline button

me

Maybe there are too many pictures on the mailbox sign. Let's cut the bird.

Word

AppleWorks

Kid Pix

7. Click on the bird.

8. Click on the **Cut** button.

Wow! The bird disappears!

9. Click on the **Save** button.

 Quick Check

Our work is done for now! Thanks for helping me make a mailbox sign.

5191
Mouse

 On Your Own

Think of something you can add to your sign. Add one more picture. Maybe you could add an animal.

Side Trips with Bernie and Blueberry

Language Arts

Write Make your own name poem. Write it just like Jess's poem. Open your word processor. Write a poem about yourself. Use different colors. Make the letters and words different sizes. Add clip art. Save it as *my poem11*. Print your poem. Share it with your class.

Science

Write Have you ever heard of the blue whale? Is it really blue? Why do zebras have stripes? Go to the library and find a book about an animal. Type a poem about it. You can use different font sizes and colors!

Professor Keys' Typing Activities

Open your word processor. Key the drill lines.

vowels

1 to   if   as   he   it   at   air   eat

2 to   if   as   he   it   at   air   eat

j, k emphasis

3 jar   ask   jet   kid   jail   kind

4 jar   ask   jet   kid   jail   kind

top row emphasis

5 air   lair   here   their   tooth

6 air   lair   here   their   tooth

n emphasis

7 on   fin   ten   noon   nine   none

8 on   fin   ten   noon   nine   none

all letters learned

9 torn   jade   look   fish   their

10 torn   jade   look   fish   their

Professor Keys' Typing Activities

Open your word processor. Key the drill lines.

Key: w

all letters learned

1 g ak is jd fe ni to rh ug

2 g ak is jd fe ni to rh ug

w emphasis

3 sw sw wsw wsw wi wj lw kw

4 sw sw wsw wsw wi wj lw kw

5 was was | will will | saw saw

6 was was | will will | saw saw

7 we we | wash wash | wilt wilt

8 we we | wash wash | wilt wilt

all letters learned

9 week soil jade fund right

10 week soil jade fund right

Side Trips with Bernie and Blueberry

Social Studies

Find Out People live in many kinds of houses. Some people in the desert live in tents. Some people live in cabins. Some people live in skyscrapers. Find clip art of different houses. Make a poster. Share your poster with your class. Tell what each house is.

Art

Make a Sign Make a mailbox sign for where you live. Type in the house number. Type your last name. Make them really big. Add some pictures. Copy one picture and paste it somewhere else on your mailbox sign. Save it as *my mailbox7*.

Quick Check

- Did you center the title?
- Did you use the **Font Size** button to make the letters in my name bigger?
- Did you use the **Font Color** button to change the color of the letters?

Follow the same steps to color the rest of the words in my poem!

Look at what I have done to my poem. It looks great!

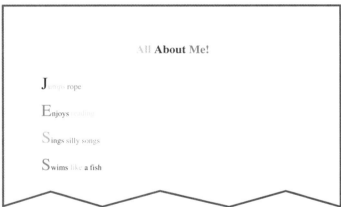

All **About Me!**

Jumps rope

Enjoys reading

Sings silly songs

Swims like a fish

On Your Own

Add a picture to go with the poem. Look for clip art that goes with one of my favorite things.

Build a House

In this project you will:

- Use the draw tools
- Use the Copy and Paste buttons
- Add color

Word Power

Copy button

Line tool

Paste button

Rectangle tool

Part 4

Color My World!

My poem looks great! But I think it needs some color. Let's make each letter in my name a different color.

1. Select the letter *J*. It is on the first line.
2. Click on the **Font Color** button arrow.
3. Click on a blue color.

Good work! I want you to change the color of the other letters in my name. Choose any color that you like. Change the color of the letters *E, S*, and *S*.

Now let's add color to the title.

4. Select the title.
5. Change the color of the title. Click on any color that you like.
6. Click on the **Save** button.

Good job!
My poem looks
beautiful!

You can even make each word of the title a different color! Try it!

All About Me!

Jumps rope

Enjoys reading

Sings silly songs

Swims like a fish

Make a House

I am learning how to draw pictures on the computer. You can draw pictures, too! Let's draw a house together. We will have fun!

Part I

Let's Begin

Let's start by opening our program.

1. Double-click on the desktop icon.

Word **AppleWorks** **Kid Pix**

AppleWorks

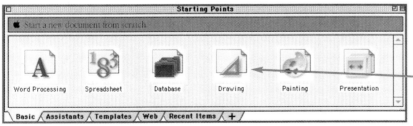

Click on the **Drawing** program.

7. Select the letter *S*. It is on the third line.

8. Click on the **Font Size** button arrow.

9. Select the font size *24*.

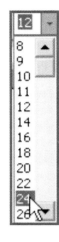

10. Select the letter *S*. It is on the last line.

11. Click on the **Font Size** button arrow.

12. Select the font size *24*.

13. Save your work.

Way to go! Now you can really see the letters in my name! The poem should look like this.

*Click on the **Save** button on the toolbar.*

All About Me!

J umps rope

E njoys reading

S ings silly songs

S wims like a fish

You might see a window like this.

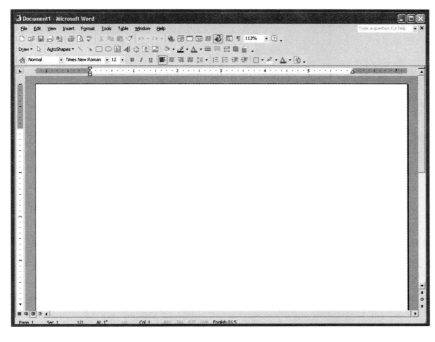

2. Click on the **Save** button on your toolbar.

Word

AppleWorks

Kid Pix

3. Type *house8* in the **File name** box.

4. Click on the **Save** button.

Jake's Ergonomics Tip

Look away from the monitor every once in a while. Look at something on the other side of the room. Blink your eyes very fast and let them rest.

Make It Big!

My poem looks nice, but we can make it better. I want to make the letters bigger. The different kinds of letters are called fonts. There are many different fonts. Let's change the font size.

Do you see my name in the poem? You are right! The letters of my name are the first letter on each line. I want to change the size of the letters in my name. Then they will show up better. I could use your help!

1. Select the letter *J*. It is on the first line.
2. Click on the **Font Size** button arrow.
3. Select the font size *24*.

Good work! Let's do that again.

4. Select the letter *E*. It is on the second line.
5. Click on the **Font Size** button arrow.
6. Select the font size *24*.

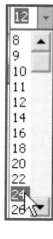

My House

Let's draw a big square for the house.

1. Click on the **Rectangle** tool.
2. Put your cursor near the middle of the page.
3. Hold down the **Shift** key and draw a big square.

Now let's add a front door.

4. Click on the **Rectangle** tool.
5. Put your cursor in the middle of the square.
6. Draw a long rectangle.
7. Click on the shape and drag it to where you want it.
8. Click on the **Save** button.

In Kid Pix, draw the shape where you want it to go. You do not have handles to move and resize the shapes!

 **Quick Check**

Do your shapes look like this? Great!

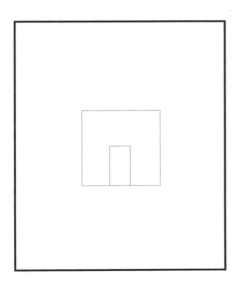

Front and Center!

Now I will show you how to put the title in the middle of the page. Look on your toolbar. You will see buttons that look like this.

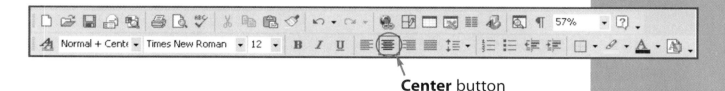

Center button

Find the Center button. Do you see it? Great! First we will select the title. We have done this before, remember? Just click and drag the mouse across the words. Ready?

1. Select the title *All About Me!*
2. Click on the **Center** button.
3. Click anywhere on the page.
4. Click on the **Save** button on the toolbar to save your work.

Word   AppleWorks

Window Boxes

Now let's add two windows. We want one window on the left and one window on the right.

1. Click on the **Rectangle** tool.
2. Hold down the **Shift** key and draw a small square next to the door.

Use the sizing handles to make the square bigger or smaller.

Click and drag to put the square where you want it.

 Word and AppleWorks

3. Click on the square.
4. Click on the **Copy** button.
5. Put your cursor where you want the square to go.
6. Click on the **Paste** button.
7. Click and drag the square if you need to move it.
8. Click on the **Save** button.

 Kid Pix

3. Draw a square on the other side of the door.
4. Click on the **Save** button.

Let's give the file a new name!

2. Choose **Save As** from the **File** menu.
3. Type *poem11* in the **File name** box.
4. Click on the **Save** button.

Choose **Save As** from the **File** menu.

Type *poem11* here.

*You do not have to type the whole file name again. Just click at the end of the word poem. Type the number 11. Then click on the **Save** button.*

Great! Now we can get started!

Jake's Ergonomics Tip

Your fingers and hands can get tired when you use the mouse. Try this! Make a tight fist. Hold it for one second. Now, spread your fingers out as far as you can. STRETCH those fingers! Hold them like that for five seconds. Now let go. Do this five times.

 **Quick Check**

Does your house look something like this?

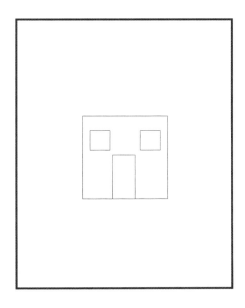

Part 4

A Roof Over My Head

Now let's add a roof.

1. Click on the **Line** tool.
2. Draw a slanted line up to make one side of the roof. Click.
3. Click on the **Line** tool again.
4. Draw a slanted line down to make the other side. Click.
5. Click on the **Save** button.

> *If you have a* ***Triangle*** *tool, you can use it to draw the roof. Try it!*

Make a Poem Pretty

I wrote a poem. I love colors, so I want to add color to the words. I can change the way the words look, too. I can make the letters bigger. I can teach you how! Let's open my poem. Follow me!

Part I

All About Me!

I wrote a poem about things I like to do. The title of my poem is "All About Me!" First let's open the file. Let's get started!

1. Double-click on the *poem* icon on the desktop.

If you cannot find the poem icon, ask your teacher.

 **Quick Check**

Your house should look something like this.

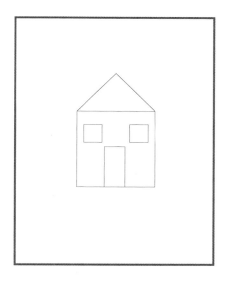

Part 5

Paint the House!

Let's add color to the house. Find the tool that lets you add color.

Word

**Fill
Color**
tool

AppleWorks

 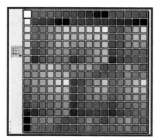

**Color
Palette**
button

Kid Pix

 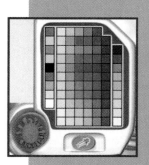

**Color
Picker**
tool

Color My World

In this project you will:

- Center text
- Change font size
- Change font color

Word Power

Center button

font

font size

toolbar

1. Click on the house.
2. Click on the black arrow in the tool to add color.
3. Click on a blue color.

4. Click on the door.
5. Click on the black arrow in the tool to add color.
6. Click on a red color.

7. Click on a window.

In Kid Pix, click on the color first. Then click on the shape!

Follow the same steps to add color to the windows. Make them light blue.

8. Click on the **Save** button.

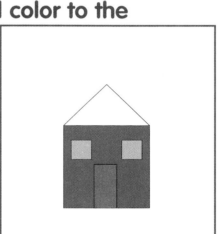

 Quick Check

Does your house look something like this?

On Your Own

Add another shape to your house. Fill the shape with a color. Have fun!

Side Trips with Bernie and Blueberry

Language Arts

Write Think about an animal story. Find two or three pictures on the computer of animals in the story. Put each animal picture on a new line. Type a sentence under each picture that tells something about the story. Print the page.

Science

Find Out Find out more about another animal. Where does it live? What does it eat? Find clip art of the animal. Put the picture of the animal on a page. Print your page. Hold up your picture and tell your classmates about this animal.

Professor Keys' Typing Activities

Open your word processor. Key the drill lines.

Key: u

all letters learned

1 h je kr lt if od ns ha ne

2 h je kr lt if od ns ha ne

u emphasis

3 ju ju uju ujk un ud uo ui

4 ju ju uju ujk un ud uo ui

5 u | due due | fun fun | use use

6 u | due due | fun fun | use use

7 rush rush | turn turn | usual

8 rush rush | turn turn | usual

all letters learned

9 ask for the nut rail jade

10 ask for the nut rail jade

Professor Keys' Typing Activities

Open your word processor. Key the drill lines.

all letters learned

1 fog   let   sun   the   jars   kind

2 fog   let   sun   the   jars   kind

3 jug   ton   hat   for   desk   fail

4 jug   ton   hat   for   desk   fail

5 lake   dish   fort   join   guide

6 lake   dish   fort   join   guide

7 joke   rule   sand   find   right

8 joke   rule   sand   find   right

9 gold   half   lake   true   joins

10 gold   half   lake   true   joins

Side Trips with Bernie and Blueberry

Art

Draw Open your word processor or drawing program. Draw a picture of a boat. Use different shapes to make your boat. Fill each shape with a color. Save your file as *my boat8*.

Language Arts

Draw Open your word processing program. Write two sentences about a pet you want. Draw the pet. Use the draw tools. Add color to the pet. Save your file as *my pet8*.

Part 4

Close the Window

You have saved the story. Now you can close the word processor.

1. Click on the **Close** box.

Word

AppleWorks

You have done a great job! Thanks for helping me with my story!

 ## On Your Own

Have you ever had a bad day? What happened on your bad day? Type your story. Add a title. You can also add a picture! Do not forget to save your work.

Sailing to America

In this project you will:

- Open a file
- Use the Backspace key
- Use the arrow keys
- Change the font color

Word Power

arrow keys

Backspace key

delete

Wonderful! Now let's look at the clip art. Does it fit? You can make it bigger or smaller.

1. Click on the picture.

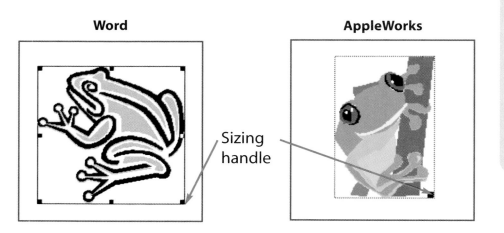

Word

AppleWorks

Sizing handle

Dragging the mouse to the right makes the picture bigger. Dragging the mouse to the left makes the picture smaller.

We will use the sizing handle to change the size of the picture.

2. Place your cursor on the sizing handle in the lower right-hand corner.

The cursor arrow changes to a sizing arrow when you move it to one of the sizing handles.

3. Click and drag the mouse to make the picture smaller.
4. Click on the **Save** button.

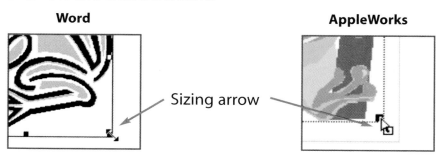

Word

AppleWorks

Sizing arrow

Fix a List

My classmates and I are learning about Christopher Columbus. He discovered America! What do you think he brought with him on his ship? We made a list. Then I hit the Time Machine button! I am back in time with Christopher Columbus. He is very nice! He looked at our list. We need to take out some of the things on the list. Can you help me? Let's go!

Part I

Set Sail

First, we need to open the file that has the list of words.

Word   AppleWorks

1. Double-click on the file named *list* to open it.

This is the list we made.

Read the list aloud with your class.

> water
>
> compass
>
> radio
>
> food
>
> maps
>
> cell phone
>
> rope
>
> candles
>
> flashlight
>
>
> Christopher Columbus found North America.

 ## Quick Check

Great! The story has a picture!

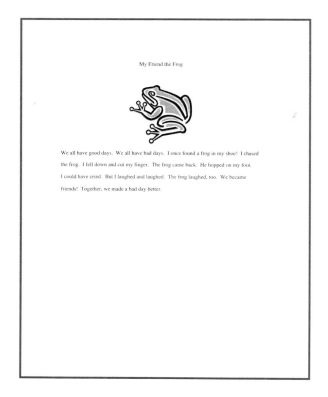

My Friend the Frog

We all have good days. We all have bad days. I once found a frog in my shoe! I chased the frog. I fell down and cut my finger. The frog came back. He hopped on my foot. I could have cried. But I laughed and laughed. The frog laughed, too. We became friends! Together, we made a bad day better.

Jake's Ergonomics Tip

How are you sitting at the computer? Your feet should be flat on the floor. Is your back against the back of your chair? Great! Now you have got it!

Let's save the list with a new name.

2. Select the **File** menu and choose **Save As**.

3. Type *list9* in the **File name** box.

4. Click on the **Save** button.

Choose **Save As** from the **File** menu.

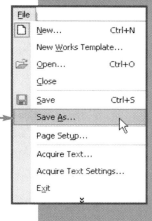

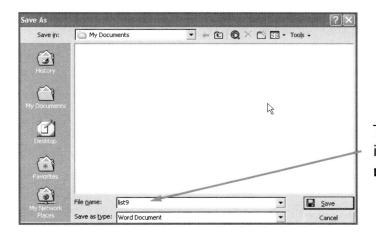

Type *list9* in the **File name** box.

You do not have to type the whole word. You can click at the end of the word list. *Now type the number 9.*

Part 2

No Phones on Board

Columbus told me that he did not take a radio on his ship. Help me take this word off the list. We can use the Backspace key.

1. Click at the end of the word *radio*.

2. Tap the **Backspace** key five times.

radio|

What other words should we delete from our list? You are right! He did not have a cell phone. We will take it off of our list.

2. Click in the search box.

3. Type *frog*.

Word

Type *frog* in the **Search for** box.

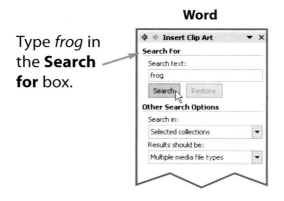

Word

AppleWorks

Type *frog* in the **Search** box.

4. Click on the **Search** button.

5. Double-click on a picture you like.

6. Click on the **Save** button.

Project 10 **94**

This time we will use the arrow keys to move to the word.

3. Tap the **Down** arrow key to move to the words *cell phone*.

4. Tap the **Right** arrow key to move to the end of the word *phone*.

5. Tap the **Backspace** key until all the letters in *cell phone* are gone.

Super! You can really move around fast!

Just one more change. Let's go!

6. Use the **Down** arrow key to move to the word *flashlight*.

7. Tap the **Right** arrow key to move to the end of the word *flashlight*.

8. Tap the **Backspace** key until all the letters in the word are gone.

9. Click on the **Save** button to save your work.

> *When we take out words on the computer, we say that we delete them!*

Jake's Ergonomics Tip

When you use a computer, remember to sit up straight in your chair. This will keep your shoulders and neck from getting stiff.

Quick Check

The story should look like this. Does it? Change it now if it does not.

> My Friend the Frog
>
> We all have good days. We all have bad days. I once found a frog in my shoe! I chased the frog. I fell down and cut my finger. The frog came back. He hopped on my foot. I could have cried. But I laughed and laughed. The frog laughed, too. We became friends! Together, we made a bad day better.

Part 3

Add a Picture!

You can add a picture to the story. Come on! I will help you!

Put your cursor under your title.

1. Click on the clip art button.

Word

AppleWorks

 **Quick Check**

Great job! Your list should look like this. If it does not, make your changes now.

> water
> compass
>
> food
> maps
>
> rope
> candles
>
>
> Christopher Columbus found North America.

Part 3

Color My World!

Read the sentence at the end of the list. Let's add color to the words that name a person or a place. These words start with a capital letter.

1. Double-click on the word *Christopher*.

Christopher Columbus found North America.

All in a Frog Day!

Every story needs a title. A title is the name of a story. It tells something about the story. I named my story *My Friend the Frog.*

1. Click at the top of the page.
2. Type the title, *My Friend the Frog.*

Now let's center the title. *Center* means "to put it in the middle."

3. Click and drag the mouse across the title to select it.

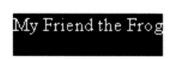

4. Click on the **Center** button on the toolbar.
5. Click after the word *Frog* in the title.
6. Tap **Enter** two times.
7. Click on the **Save** button on the toolbar.

2. Make the letters blue.

3. Double-click on the word *Columbus*.

4. Make the letters blue.

Good! You did it! Now let's make one more change.

5. Double-click on the word *North*.

6. Make the letters green.

7. Double-click on the word *America*.

8. Make the letters green.

9. Save your work.

Wonderful! You have been a big help!

*To add color click on the arrow by the **Font Color** or **Text Color** button. Now select the color!*

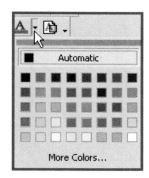

On Your Own

Can you think of other things Columbus might have taken with him? Add them to your list. Save it as *my list9*. Print the list. Draw a picture of Christopher Columbus on the page. Take the list home and show it to your family.

Let's give the story a new name.

2. Choose **Save As** from the **File** menu.

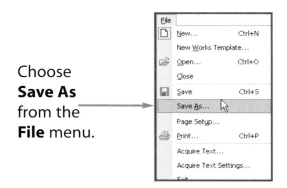

Choose
Save As
from the
File menu.

You should see a window like this one.

Type
story10 in
the **File name** box.

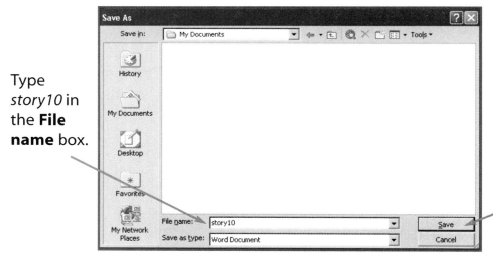

Click on
Save.

3. Click at the end of the word *story* in the **File name** box.

4. Type *10*.

5. Click on the **Save** button.

Great job! You have saved the file with a new name.

Professor Keys' Typing Activities

Open your word processor. Key the drill lines.

Key: g

all letters learned

1 u fe ra ts nd ul ij ok nh

2 u fe ra ts nd ul ij ok nh

g emphasis

3 fg fg gfg gfg gh gk gj gn

4 fg fg gfg gfg gh gk gj gn

5 gift gift | eggs eggs | grand

6 gift gift | eggs eggs | grand

phrases

7 go get it | green fog light

8 go get it | green fog light

all letters learned

9 tug old ski jar the found

10 tug old ski jar the found

Write a Story

We all have good days. We all have bad days. I once found a frog in my shoe! I chased the frog. I fell down and cut my finger. The frog came back. He hopped on my foot.

I could have cried. But I laughed and laughed. The frog laughed, too. We became friends! Together, we made a bad day better. Will you help me write a story about my bad day? I will help you get started!

Part I

A Fresh Start

We need to open the story. We will use an icon. I will tell you how!

1. Double-click on the *story* icon on your desktop.

Word

story

AppleWorks

story

Side Trips with Bernie and Blueberry

Social Studies

List Learn more about Christopher Columbus. Who did he meet? What things did he find? Find facts in books from your library or classroom. Open your word processor. Make a list of some things you learned. Make the words different colors. Save it as *my facts9*.

Language Arts

List What do you bring with you when you go on a trip? Type a list of the things you bring. Then put the words in different colors. Save it as *my trip9*.

Good Days and Bad Days

In this project you will:

- Open a file
- Insert text
- Center text
- Add a picture
- Resize a picture
- Save a file
- Close a program

Word Power

center

clip art

icon

GLOSSARY

A

add to combine numbers to get a total

address the location where an e-mail message is sent

arrow keys keys on the keyboard that can be used to move the cursor on the screen

B

Back button a button on an Internet toolbar that helps you move back to a page that you have already seen

Backspace key a key on the keyboard used to erase the letter, number, or symbol one space to the left of the cursor

Bold button a button on the toolbar that makes letters dark

button a spot that you click on your computer screen to tell the computer to do something

C

cable an electrical cord that connects parts of a computer system together

CD-ROM a round, shiny disk that holds information

cell a box in a spreadsheet, occurring where a column and a row meet

center to put text in the middle of an area

clip art pictures and designs that can be added to a document

Color palette button a draw tool that will fill a shape with color

Color Picker tool a drawing tool that adds color to an area

column an up and down arrangement of boxes on a spreadsheet, usually labeled with a letter

column heading a label or words used to name a column in a spreadsheet

computer a machine that processes information

copy to make the exact same thing to put in another place in the document

Copy button a button used to copy words to move them

CPU (Central Processing Unit) the hardware that enables computers to store and use data

cursor a blinking line on a screen that shows where the next typed letter, number, or symbol will appear

cut to remove words or pictures so they can be put in a different place

Cut button a button used to cut text or pictures

D

data information such as words, numbers, or pictures

database information stored in a computer and organized as records

delete to erase

Delete key a key on the keyboard used to erase words or pictures

desktop the background on a computer screen

document also called a file; pages, such as a letter or a report, created on a computer

draw tools tools used to draw shapes, such as lines, circles, and squares

E

edit to change words or pictures

e-mail electronic mail; messages that are sent and received by computers

enter to insert words

Enter key a key on the right side of the keyboard that will begin a new paragraph or tell the computer program to do something

F

field a place where information, such as a name or address, is entered in a database

file also called a document; pages, such as a letter or a report, created on a computer

File menu the pull-down menu under *File*

Fill Color tool a drawing tool used to add color to an area

Fill tool a paint tool used to add color to an object

floppy disk a thin disk that stores information

font the style of letters, numbers, and symbols in a document

Font button a button on the toolbar used to choose a font

Font Color button a button on the toolbar that changes the color of letters

font size the size of letters, numbers, and symbols

Font Size button a button on the toolbar used to choose the size of a font

format to change the font style, color, size, and font

Forward button a button on an Internet toolbar that helps you move forward to the next page

G

graphic a picture, drawing, or design

H

hardware the parts of a computer system such as the keyboard, monitor, and computer case

heading the title at the top of a column or side of a row

home page the first page of a Web site

hyperlink a word or picture that connects one Web page with another

I

icon a picture that stands for a file or folder

Inbox a folder where e-mail messages are received and stored

insert to add letters, words, or other information in a document

Internet a large network of computers that connects computers all over the world

Internet browser a program that allows computer users to move from one Web site to another within the Internet

Internet toolbar a row of command buttons across the top of an Internet page

Italic button a button on the toolbar that makes letters slanted

K

keyboard a set of keys used to type letters, numbers, and symbols into the computer

L

layout the way that text and images are arranged on a page

Line tool a draw tool used to draw lines on a page

link a word or picture that connects one Web page with another

M

menu a list of commands that tell the computer what to do

monitor a machine that shows computer information on a screen

mouse an object moved across the top of a desk that controls the cursor or pointer on the computer screen

O

offline not connected to the Internet

online connected to the Internet

Outbox a folder where e-mail messages are stored until they are sent

Oval tool a draw or paint tool used to draw circles and ovals on a page

P

paste to insert cut or copied text in a document

Paste button a button on the toolbar used to insert cut or copied text in a document

printer a machine that prints a document created on a computer

program the instructions inside a computer that tell it what to do

pull-down menu also called a drop-down menu; a list of commands in a program

R

record a group of fields about one topic in a database

Rectangle tool a draw or paint tool used to draw squares or rectangles on a page

resize to make something larger or smaller

Return a key on the right side of the keyboard that will start a new paragraph

right-click to click on the right side of the mouse button

row an arrangement of boxes across a spreadsheet, usually labeled with numbers

row heading a label or words used to name a row in a spreadsheet

S

Save As to save a file with a different name

screen the part of the monitor that you look at when you work on your computer

scroll bar a bar along the side or bottom of a window that shows if the whole window is seen

select to highlight text to change it

Shift key a key to hold down with another key when you want to make a capital letter

sizing handles the points on a graphic used to make the graphic bigger or smaller

software a computer program that tells the computer what to do

Space Bar the long bar at the bottom of the keyboard that you use when you want to add a space between letters

speakers part of the computer that sends out sound

spelling checker a tool that finds and corrects misspelled words in a document

spreadsheet a software program that works with numbers

spreadsheet cursor a blinking cross-shaped character that shows where the next typed letter, number, or symbol will appear on a spreadsheet

store to save information on a disk

style the way typed words look, such as bold, italicized, or underlined

T

Tab key a key used to move from cell to cell in a spreadsheet. The Tab key will also indent copy.

table information that is shown in rows and columns

Text Color button a button on the toolbar that adds color to an area

text insertion point the blinking line on the screen where the next typed letter, number, or symbol will appear

Text tool a tool used to add text to pictures on a page

toolbar a row of command buttons across the top of a software program; clicking a toolbar button is a shortcut for using the menu commands

U

Underline button a button on the toolbar that underlines words

W

Web address the location of a Web site on the Internet

Web page a document on the Internet with text, graphics, sound, and video that can link to other Web pages

Web site a group of related Web pages, images, and other files

word processing program a software program used to create and edit documents

wrap to place words around a graphic image in a document

WWW (World Wide Web) a part of the Internet that has Web pages with links to other Web pages

Z

Zoom button a button that makes a window larger or smaller